Robert E. Wells

Bookcraft
Salt Lake City, Utah

Library of Congress Catalog Card Number: 82-74412
ISBN O-88494-477-8

First Printing, 1983

Lithographed in the United States of America
PUBLISHERS PRESS
Salt Lake City, Utah

To my dear wife, Helen

CONTENTS

Can God Trust You?

Before coming into full-time service as a General Authority, I spent many years as a banker in Latin America. This was followed by a period of Church service in a somewhat related field. These experiences have often caused me to ponder the facts that *trust* is a two-way street and that it involves all aspects of our lives, both temporal and spiritual. The borrower must trust the lender, and both must be worthy of trust. The Church leader must trust the stewards assigned to him, and both must be worthy of trust. Those who put up their petitions to the Lord are also those whom the Lord must trust to do his work here on this particular kind of a mortal planet that he designed. Otherwise, he would have to change his own rules. So we, too, must be worthy of his trust.

Trustworthiness is an element of human greatness, and when a person has become in all respects worthy of God's trust, he has made himself worthy of man's. Many are the stories indicating the high trust in which the Saints held the Prophet Joseph. This one is by Sarah M. Pomeroy.

My father moved from New York to Nauvoo in the spring of 1843. I was then in my ninth year. The day after our arrival I was out in the yard when a gentleman rode up and inquired for my father, Thomas Colborn. Of course I did not know who it was, but there was something so noble and dignified in his appearance that it struck me forcibly.

My father soon came out and cordially shook him by the hand, and called him Brother Joseph. I knew then it was the Prophet.

It was quite an exciting time just then. The Prophet had been falsely accused of an attempt to murder Governor Boggs of Missouri. Porter Rockwell, a firm friend of Joseph, had been kidnapped and taken to Missouri as an accomplice, and was about to have his trial. Joseph requested my father to lend him a hundred dollars to pay the lawyer who defended Porter Rockwell, and father freely counted out the money.

"This shall be returned within three days, if I am alive," said the Prophet, and departed.

My aunt, Father's sister, was quite wrathful. "Don't you know, Thomas," said she, "you will never see a cent of that money again. Here are your family without a home, and you throw your money away."

"Don't worry, Katie," Father replied, "if he cannot pay it, he is welcome to it."

This conversation was held before us children, and I thought seriously about it. Would he pay it, or would he not? But I had strong faith that he would.

The day came when it was to be paid—a cold, wet, rainy day. The day passed. Night came—9 o'clock, 10 o'clock, and we all retired for the night. Shortly after there was a knock at the door. Father arose and went to it, and there in the driving rain stood the Prophet Joseph.

"Here, Brother Thomas, is the money." A light was struck, and he counted out the hundred dollars in gold.

He said, "Brother Thomas, I have been trying all day to raise this sum, for my honor was at stake. God bless you." (Hyrum L. Andrus and Helen Mae Andrus, *They Knew the Prophet*, Bookcraft, 1974, pp. 171-72.)

All trustworthiness is based on preparation. If we would be worthy of God's trust—that is, be useful to him—we must prepare. Part of that preparation will be voluntary and deliberate. As a covenant people, we commit ourselves to the Lord and his cause, and to the extent that we honor that commitment he can trust us with greater responsibility—even, perhaps, with greater trials and tests for our further growth and development. All this, even the involuntary trials, is a part of our preparation in trustworthiness as well as a stimulus to increasing our trust in the Lord.

We find many examples of this process in Church history. In early days, ostracism and persecution was a common price paid for accepting the gospel. Within a very few years, thousands had been uprooted from their homes several times as they passed through the fiery tests of Missouri and Illinois. Then in 1846 it was the cold, weary trek across Iowa. The Saints who were in Winter Quarters or other places across Iowa as 1847 dawned had been well tested and prepared as to both their trust in God and their trustworthiness.

In early April of that year the initial pioneer company of 148 people set off from Winter Quarters on the thousand-mile trek to the Great Basin area, where they would arrive in late July. We rightly honor that first company for their courage and faith and their trust in God. It is true that 143 members of the company were capable, strong men largely in the prime of life. It is true that Brigham Young and other leaders had a map or two and a general idea of the nature of their destination. But far more significant was the basic equipment of trust in God—trust that he would sustain the company in their journey, lead them to the precise destination, and then help them and the oncoming thousands to support life and build a community in a far-from-fertile land.

On June 21, that first company had reached Independence Rock, about 175 miles west of Fort Laramie. I am impressed by the fact that *on that same day, more than a month before they had reached their as yet unknown destination,* another company set out from Winter Quarters led by Elders Parley P. Pratt and John Taylor. This large company contained 1553 people, 2213 oxen, 887 cows, and 124 horses, plus other livestock. If the first company merits our admiration at these qualities, what should we say of the trust and trustworthiness this second group displayed?

Here is what B. H. Roberts wrote of them:

> This company differed from the pioneers. The latter was made up of able-bodied men, excepting three women—none were helpless. They had the best of teams, and if they failed in finding a place of settlement they could return to the place of starting. Meantime their families were not endangered. They were secure at Winter Quarters. Not so with the Pratt and Taylor company. They had their all upon the altar, including their wives and children, who must share their hardships and their fate. They knew not their destination, they entrusted all on a single venture, from which there was no chance of retreat. If they should fail to find a suitable location and raise a crop the first season, there was no getting provisions to them, nor them to provisions. They must succeed, or perish in the wilderness to which they had started. With a faith that has never been surpassed, they placed themselves under the guidance and protection of their God, and . . . they trusted not in vain. (*The Life of John Taylor,* Bookcraft, 1963, pp. 188-89.)

All this represents part of the preparation we have described as involuntary. On the voluntary side, not only preparation by commitment to righteousness is required but also preparation by gaining knowledge and developing skills. Every good thing you ever learn, every preparation for life you ever make, will be used some day. In fact, you can just about determine what your opportunities to serve will be by what you learn or by what you refuse to learn. Of course, if you lack a zest for life that will get you involved in sports and such things as learning to fly a plane, you will be somewhat limited. And if you avoid getting acquainted with people and do not reach out to them, this will limit you.

For each of us there is perhaps a particular situation wherein we are precisely the right person for the Lord to trust. Trust is a two-way street. The Lord can trust you if you have become trustworthy. You can, of course, always trust the Lord if you will. And you will if you have made yourself, with the help of the Lord, into a trusting person.

So there are two qualities of trust that you may wish to develop. The one is becoming trustworthy—having the qualities that will cause others to perceive you as a person they need and can use. The second quality of trust you may want is the quality of trusting—that is, being able to act like David when he faced Goliath.

All the Israelites had been taught that the true God was the God of Israel. The idols of Egypt and Philistia could not be depended upon, but Jehovah would not fail if trust was pure. David's trust was pure. Saul's was not. And Saul's captains and mighty men did not trust the Lord as David trusted the Lord. So David did not go forward with halting steps, quavering lips, and a fear-filled heart. He "hasted" to meet Goliath. He ran toward this fearsome giant.

And the outcome was just as David expected: The Lord delivered Goliath into David's hand. David was just the trusting instrument. He felt trust in his heart. He was prepared. He was well practiced with the sling. He had previous experience of boldness in action and had slain wild animals in protecting his father's flocks. He was the right man in the right place, and the Lord could use him.

I suppose that most have no vision of what the Lord could do with them if they would fully trust him and put themselves at his disposal and say, "We'll do whatever you wish, and you can do to us whatever you wish." Brigham Young, in many of his speeches, talked about how great the Saints could become if they totally trusted the Lord. He said that nearly all of us put a limit on God and will not lay ourselves completely at his feet for fear he will take away "our little ones" or our riches.

One of the greatest elements of trust is the ability to take each step forward even if it is into the dark and unknown. (Remember, the Lord didn't part the Red Sea until Moses and the children of Israel had no other place to put their feet.) Then the Lord can lead you to wherever he wants you to serve and make you into whatever he wants to make you. And that will bring you the greatest happiness in the long run, because the Lord wants us all to become like him and have what he has.

If you wish to have a useful and productive life and become worthy of great trust in all your pursuits, learn to drive both ways on the two-way street of trust. That is, learn to trust the Lord and to discipline yourself into the mold of trustworthiness.

CHAPTER TWO

The Three Cs of Trust

On one side of all United States coins and currency is the legend "In God we trust." It is an echo out of our more Christian past and a feeble attempt to declare that, while money is essential to commerce, we really trust God, not money. Would that this were truly and totally the case! Even more, would that the other side of the coin could be truthfully inscribed "And God can trust us"! For there are two sides to the coin of trust. And the furtherance of righteousness is effectively immobilized if either side is missing.

Note that we (each and all of us) are the unknown quantity or variable in this equation. The Lord absolutely and always can be trusted; but we also must be willing to trust (the one side of the coin) and be worthy of trust (the other side of the coin) if humanity is to be blessed. That is one of the laws the Lord gave this world by which it was to operate. (See D&C 88: 36-43.) He could do everything for us; but that would defeat his purposes. So the manifestations of his blessings and goodness usually come through us, and they come in the proportion that we trust him and are trustworthy.

The Lord wants us to trust him. He also wants us to become trustworthy so he can trust us to do his work. A main purpose of this life is to prove us: "And we will prove them herewith, to see if they will do all things whatsoever the Lord their God shall command them." (Abraham 3:25.) President David O. McKay often repeated a favorite quotation about it being greater to be trusted than to be loved. Whoever first said that was blessed with a great insight into how life works. God loves all; but he can save only those who can be trusted, just as a banker can extend credit only to those he can trust, no matter how much he may love those he cannot trust.

The Prophet Joseph Smith pointed out the necessity to be thoroughly tested to demonstrate that the Lord can trust us in all circumstances. He said:

> After a person has faith in Christ, repents of his sins, and is baptized for the remission of his sins and receives the Holy Ghost, (by the laying on of hands), which is the first Comforter, then let him continue to humble himself before God, hungering and thirsting after righteousness, and living by every word of God, and the Lord will soon say unto him, Son, thou shalt be exalted. When the Lord has thoroughly proved him, and finds that the man is determined to serve Him at all hazards, then the man will find his calling and his election made sure. (*History of the Church*, vol. 3, p. 380.)

This testing and the sacrifice it entails, the Prophet taught, is a prerequisite to eternal life.

> Let us here observe, that a religion that does not require the sacrifice of all things never has power sufficient to produce the faith necessary unto life and salvation; for, from the first existence of man, the faith necessary unto the enjoyment of life and salvation never could be obtained without the sacrifice of all earthly things. It was through this sacrifice, and this only, that God has ordained that men should enjoy eternal life. (*Lectures on Faith* 6:7.)

The Lord loves all of his children, but some are more trustworthy than others. Love is a quality of the one who loves and, once developed, is given regardless of the worth of the object of that love. But only fools trust those who are not worthy of trust; because that is the road to disaster. Wouldn't it be marvelous to be *both* loved and trusted? The gospel and the Church are given to us by the Lord as the means of achieving that goal.

It has often been said that a better measure of a man's true worth than what he possesses is what he can borrow—that is, how far he can be trusted with other people's money. Bankers have a formula for determining whom they can trust with the bank's money. I believe this formula has a direct application to spiritual or moral trust. In fact,

I can't see how one can separate a person's integrity into a Church pile and a business pile. Inevitably we treat the Lord's assets in just about the same way we treat our own. Among Church members, one test the Lord uses to determine trustworthiness in the kingdom is trustworthiness in personal affairs. Jesus said,

> And I say unto you, Make to yourselves friends of the mammon of unrighteousness; that, when ye fail, they may receive you into everlasting habitations.
>
> He that is faithful in that which is least is faithful also in much: and he that is unjust in the least is unjust also in much.
>
> If therefore ye have not been faithful in the unrighteous mammon, who will commit to your trust the true riches?
>
> And if ye have not been faithful in that which is another man's, who shall give you that which is your own? (Luke 16:9-12.)

Bear in mind that the above passage has eternal ramifications as well as temporal ones.

The banker's formula for determining whether to trust someone with his bank's money is to look at the loan applicant's *character, capacity,* and *capital.* At least, he must try to assess these three qualities or assets. In an analogous way, the Lord looks at these three qualities in determining ultimate blessings and trust.

The Lord's servants also must look at these three basic qualities, as far as ability and information will allow, in their search for leadership in the great work of the kingdom. You may not realize it, but nearly everyone in the Church is considered in leadership meetings during any given year. They are discussed always in kindness, with great sympathy and understanding for whatever problems they have. But one of the main reasons why their names are mentioned is that Church leaders on all levels are engaged in this never-ending search for leadership. To a great extent, leadership means trustworthy and trusting people. So these leadership searches are thoughtful and prayerful appraisals of the *character, capacity,* and *capital* of ward and branch members. You might say that the spiritual bankers are holding a "loan meeting" to determine who is worthy of a spiritual loan.

The temporal banker is a steward of money he doesn't usually own, but for which he is responsible. So he must take every precaution he reasonably can to lend only to those who can and will repay. The spiritual banker is a steward of the good name of the church that bears our Savior's name. That name must not be shamed or defamed before the world. So the Church stewards must take every reasonable precaution to call to positions only those who can be trusted to hold sacred the name of Christ's church. And if you will be realistic and honest, you will have to admit that for the most part they do a very good job.

A banker has to look at a loan applicant's *character* in much the same terms that David uses in Psalm 15:

> Lord, who shall abide in thy tabernacle? who shall dwell in thy holy hill?
>
> He that walketh uprightly, and worketh righteousness, and speaketh the truth in his heart. . . .
>
> He that sweareth to his own hurt, and changeth not. (Verses 1-4.)

A person who borrows money swears to repay it. Sometimes the business use to which it is put fails. The crop fails. The business venture doesn't succeed. Then he has sworn "to his own hurt." Then the honest person "changeth not." He still pays off the loan as rapidly as possible. A banker must feel he is dealing with that kind of person; that is, one who will not default and make the excuse that the loan didn't help, was useless, and that paying it back creates a greater burden than was there before the loan. If there is any doubt in the banker's mind that the borrower's ethics and morals will lead him to meet his obligations no matter what the sacrifice, there will be no trust and no loan will be granted.

The Lord, of course, knows everything about us. But we do not. And it is his desire and his work and glory to bring us to eternal life and immortality and give us all that he has. So he must treat us much the same as if he were a banker trying to find out how far he can trust us. In that sense, the Lord needs to know if he can trust us to do the right thing in every situation. So he increases our "credit line" a little at a time as he tests us.

For example, Joseph, when he first was sold into Egypt, worked himself up in the service of Potiphar until he became chief steward. But the wife of Potiphar fell in love with Joseph and attempted to entice him into sin. Joseph was far from home and family. He didn't even know if he would ever see them again. No one on earth would know or care about his morals. To have capitulated to sin and the wishes of Potiphar's wife would have been an easy way out of a great dilemma. On the one hand, he was a trusted slave. True, only a slave, but a trusted slave: Potiphar had entrusted him with everything he had. On the other hand, if he spurned this woman, he would have a great enemy in his master's house.

Joseph was true to his noble character and the teachings of his father. He didn't hesitate. He fled from sin. The price was imprisonment, because Potiphar's wife accused him of attempted rape and gave as evidence the cloak he had left behind. This was a great price to pay for purity; but to have done otherwise would have demonstrated a great and tragic flaw in his character. In that case the Lord would have refused to trust him to become a savior to all Israel later on. He would have been forgotten instead of being held up by later prophets as a type of Christ.

In another classic example, Nephi's strength of character led him to obey a commandment and undertake a very dangerous assignment. He easily could have been slain by the wicked Laban when he went back to get the plates. Yet not to obey, when he had the testimony that the Lord would open the way for him to obtain the plates, would have been a flaw in his character.

The Lord proved that he could trust Joseph and Nephi. Joseph and Nephi already knew in an intellectual sense that they could trust the Lord; but their experiences taught them a new dimension of trust. (See Alma 13:3, 7.) They had to learn by experience, actually had to go through it and cement it into their characters, even as the Son of Man "learned . . . obedience by the things which he suffered." (Hebrews 5:8.) This, of course, doesn't mean that Jesus was ever disobedient. We know that he was not. But there is a dimension of knowledge that comes only with experience. It is one thing for you to have the ability to be trustworthy. It is another to have gone through the experience of having been trustworthy. Thus, there is no substitute for the particular experience that God puts each of us through.

A person of high character testifies and then lives in harmony with his testimony. Martin Luther, at the Diet of Worms, demonstrated this principle of being true to self when he said, ". . . my conscience is taken captive by God's Word, and I neither can nor will revoke anything, seeing it is not safe or right to act against conscience. God help me. Amen." (*Encyclopaedia Britannica*, 14th ed., vol. 14, p. 494.) Thereafter, Luther had to live with those words. His character required it.

When Joseph Smith compared his experience with the Apostle Paul's, he gave us a great insight into the character of both. Speaking of Paul, he said: "He saw a light, and heard a voice . . . some said he was dishonest, others said he was mad; . . . But all this did not destroy the reality of his vision. He had seen a vision, he knew he had, and all the persecution under heaven could not make it otherwise." Then Joseph Smith added this revealing testimony: "I had seen a vision; I knew it, and I knew that God knew it, and I could not deny it, neither dared I do it." (Joseph Smith—History, 1:24, 25.) Joseph Smith and the Apostle Paul were men of great and noble character whom the Lord knew he could trust no matter what the sacrifice. In both cases the sacrifice was martyrdom.

Active membership in The Church of Jesus Christ of Latter-day Saints builds a Christlike character provided all the activities are done for the right reasons. The same can be said about a full-time mission. President Harold B. Lee gave a speech at Brigham Young University many years ago in which he emphasized this idea about doing things for the right reasons. He centered this idea mostly around going on a mission. He listed many wrong reasons for going, such as to see the world, to learn a language, to satisfy the desires of parents or the girl friend, and so forth. He explained that he realized that many who go for the wrong reason, later learn and live up to the right reason while out there. But he pointed out the value of proper motivation right from the start. The right reason for all Church activity is, of course, the building up of the Lord's kingdom and the establishment of Zion. The right motivation behind this reason or desire is charity or the pure love of Christ, with which we can be filled when we have been born again and filled with the Holy Spirit. It comes as a gift of God; but we have to do our part too.

Perhaps it would be safe to say that character is the quality that requires us to do the right thing for the right reason at all times. That would be the ideal and godly state that would please both a banker and the Lord.

The *capacity* which the banker looks for in his client is that proven ability to perform as promised. Character is the intent to perform. Capacity is the ability to perform. The capacity the Lord needs in us is that ability to perform as profitable servants. The Lord has given us talents, gifts, blessings, and opportunities. He expects us to magnify them and to use them in the service of others if he is to trust us.

The servant who had received five talents returned ten and received this praise: "Well done, thou good and faithful servant: thou hast been faithful over a few things, I will make thee ruler over many things." (Matthew 25:21.) The servant who had received two talents returned four talents, and he received equal praise with the first. However, the Lord chastised the slothful servant who had received one talent for not multiplying that which had been given to him. The principle is clear: The Lord likes to see capacity doubled. He likes to see his servants double that which has been given to them, in talents or in responsibilities. It is evident that the Presidents of the Church tend, also, to want to see things doubled. They like to see double the number of missionaries, double the number of new faithful members coming into the Church, double the attendance at sacrament meeting, and so on. I believe that each one of us has a sacred responsibility to multiply our capacity and our performance in every measurable way. In so doing, we vindicate the Lord's trust in our capacity as his servants.

There are many areas besides Church service in which we could make a sustained effort to increase our capacity. We could strive to increase our technical capacity in our daily breadwinning labors. We could strive to improve our capacity as parents and teachers. We could multiply our capacity as missionaries in asking the "golden questions" and in sharing the gospel with everyone. We could improve our capacity as informed citizens, as Christian neighbors giving service to others, and so on. And all this would not only make us of greater service to the Lord, it would end up by opening doors to us that would bring us material rewards all our lives. Active membership in the Church can build both spiritual and temporal capacity. A full-time mission especially can develop capacity that the Lord can trust.

The banker looks at and lists a client's *capital* for three reasons: 1) as a reserve which the client has available to meet payments or emergencies in case he has to repay the loan out of his reserves instead of out of what he earned through the loan; 2) as a measure of the client's commitment to the venture; and 3) as an index of his total worth.

On the spiritual side of the coin, we might say that the Lord is looking for a spiritual reserve in the individual with which he can meet the emergencies that arise in the kingdom. A steward's total worth, in the best spiritual sense, refers to such things as his friendship with God and man, his active spiritual gifts, and his present state of worthiness—his freedom from vice and sin, from anything that could detract from his usefulness to the Lord or the Lord's church.

Spiritual capital, then, is the investment a person has made in righteous living. It is an asset, in reserve, upon which he may draw in time of need.

How do we develop spiritual capital and reserves? We need to make an investment in time spent studying the scriptures and the words of our living prophets; an investment in more meaningful communication with our Father in Heaven; an investment in service to others; an investment in unconditional, unselfish love of others; an investment in missionary labor which can bring blessings and forgiveness of our sins; an investment in being wiser parents or more obedient children; an investment in doubling our performance in every calling. These investments will provide such spiritual capital and reserves that the Lord can truly trust us to overcome the temptations and frustrations of the world.

Our forefathers built great spiritual reserves by investing in sacrifice. They could face any challenge because they knew that their individual lives were in order and that they were favored by Heaven because of the sacrifices they had made in giving up everything that was dear to them in order to follow the Lord through his prophets. They suffered persecutions; they went out as missionaries, leaving families behind; they left productive farms and well-built homes in the East to go out into dry western deserts or cold mountains to begin again.

Wouldn't it be wonderful if the Lord could say of all of us as he did of one particular member in a revelation given in Nauvoo in 1838: "My servant George Miller is without guile; he may be trusted because of the integrity of his heart; and for the love which he has to my testimony I, the Lord, love him." (D&C 124:20.)

The three Cs of trust are *character, capacity,* and *capital,* whether you are looking at trust temporally or spiritually. We tend to be the same in our Church assignments as we are in our workaday world. If we are not we are hypocrites. A hypocrite is an actor. He acts one role in the Church and another one out there in the world. *Hypocrite* is related etymologically to the Greek word *hypokrinesthai,* to play a part or pretend. The same word was applied to acting on a stage. Hypocrisy divides and destroys souls. We would all be wise to make our lives one and single to the glory of God. Then peace and success will come easier. Then we will know and feel trust. Like a good banker, we all ought to assess regularly our *character,* our *capacity,* and our *capital.*

CHAPTER THREE

Acceptance and Our Trust in God

As a background to succeeding chapters which will pursue further the three Cs of trust, I would like to caution readers, especially young readers, not to interpret what I have said as encouragement to seek what we often call high positions, or to swim upstream when common sense would keep you out of that particular water. If being greatest means being a servant, as Jesus taught, then greatness lies all around you right where you are. Concentrate on the service, and the Lord and his servants will take you by the hand and lead you to even greater service. But it may not be in "high" positions. On the other hand, of course, do not shirk or run from great responsibility. If we trust in God, all handicaps and obstacles will become mere signposts in the path he wishes us to take.

Reinhold Niebuhr, in a commonly used statement, said very well part of what I wish to say in this chapter:

> God, give us grace to accept with serenity the things that cannot be changed, courage to change the things which should be changed, and the wisdom to distinguish the one from the other.

This quotation evokes mental images of people in wheelchairs or led by seeing-eye dogs, and then leads the mind through the whole gamut of handicaps that come to people through accidents, heredity, and environment. By and by it conjures up such things as luck and war and the social mobility of the country into which one's body is born. At last, the mind ponders the problems of those who can become anything they want to, and only have to consider such things as God's desires on "what might be best for me."

Such a person was President Hugh B. Brown. At least, one would think he was "lucky" if his history weren't so well known. Actually he suffered great disappointments and trials. But these things come to all great people for their own good. And all suffering is relative. That is, everyone tends to suffer to a degree that is determined by what kind of a sufferer he is, not to a degree that is fixed by any absolute standard of causes for suffering. Thus, what one person might shrug off as nothing can be a great cause for suffering to another person.

When President Brown was a young missionary in England, he had a dream in which he saw himself climbing a ladder or sort of a stairway. When he was quite high up he dropped something valuable into the stairwell and he had to go to the bottom to retrieve it. Then he started climbing again and eventually got nearer to the top than ever before.

He later went to a grandmother who was spiritually gifted and asked her the meaning of the dream. She told him it meant that he would get quite high in the Church and then something would cause him to be dropped and ignored, but that he would outlive it and eventually preside in the highest councils of the Church. On a few occasions he told this story when he became a General Authority.

President Brown was called to many positions when quite young, and at forty-five he became president of a stake in the Salt Lake area. A few years later he accepted an appointment on a state commission. In this assignment he came to be subjected to the pressures of conflicting business and political forces and to an increasing atmosphere of misrepresentation and unfair criticism. In the midst of this situation he was released as stake president. This was a great trial to him. But the dream and interpretation came true. He rose to serve in the highest council of the Church. In the meantime he had a distinguished career in military service, in law, in university teaching, and in business.

I relate the foregoing as an introduction to my favorite story about accepting things that cannot or should not be changed. President Brown is the author of this story, and it was based on two episodes in his life. One was the time he was passed over for a promotion to a high rank in the Canadian army. This was shattering to him because he had determined to make the military his lifelong career. Now, he realized that it would be hard, if not impossible, for a Mormon to obtain the rank of general, because he would not drink and socialize in the manner that was considered necessary at that time and in that place. In fact, he sometimes confided that he was told as much at the time he was passed over. Years later he realized that the end of his military career was the beginning of a new direction that led to a far more useful and rewarding life than he would have had if he had gone unpruned into the fulfillment of his own early ambitions.

The other episode involves the pruning of a currant bush. In his rich imagination, President Brown saw in these two experiences what has become a great parable to many of us. I think it is worthy of repeating here because it is so appropriate to the message I wish to convey in this chapter.

The Gardener and the Currant Bush

In the early dawn, a young gardener was pruning his trees and shrubs. He had one choice currant bush which had gone too much to wood. He feared therefore that it would produce little, if any, fruit.

Accordingly, he trimmed and pruned the bush and cut it back. In fact, when he had finished, there was little left but stumps and roots.

Tenderly he considered what was left. It looked so sad and deeply hurt. On every stump there seemed to be a tear where the pruning knife had cut away the growth of early spring. The poor bush seemed to speak to him, and he thought he heard it say:

"Oh, how could you be so cruel to me; you who claim to be my friend, who planted me and cared for me when I was young, and nurtured and encouraged me to grow? Could you not see that I was rapidly responding to your care? I was nearly half as large as the trees across the fence, and might soon have become like one of them. But now you've cut my branches back; the green, attractive leaves are gone, and I am in disgrace among my fellows."

The young gardener looked at the weeping bush and heard its plea with sympathetic understanding. His voice was full of kindness as he said: "Do not cry; what I have done to you was necessary that you might be a prize currant bush in my garden. You were not intended to give shade or shelter by your branches. My purpose when I planted you was that you should bear fruit. When I want currants, a tree, regardless of its size, cannot supply the need.

"No, my little currant bush, if I had allowed you to continue to grow as you had started, all your strength would have gone to wood; your roots would not have gained a firm hold, and the purpose for which I brought you into my garden would have been defeated. Your place would have been taken by another, for you would have been barren. You must not weep; all this will be for your good; and some day, when you see more clearly, when you are richly laden with luscious fruit, you will thank me and say, 'Surely, he was a wise and loving gardener. He knew the purpose of my being, and I thank him now for what I then thought was cruelty.'"

Some years later, this young gardener was in a foreign land, and he himself was growing. He was proud of his position and ambitious for the future.

One day an unexpected vacancy entitled him to promotion. The goal to which he had aspired was now almost within his grasp, and he was proud of the rapid growth which he was making.

But for some reason unknown to him, another was appointed in his stead, and he was asked to take another post relatively unimportant and which, under the circumstances, caused his friends to feel that he had failed.

The young man staggered to his tent and knelt beside his cot and wept. He knew now that he could never hope to have what he had thought so desirable. He cried to God and said, "Oh, how could you be so cruel to me? You who claim to be my friend—you who brought me here and nurtured and encouraged me to grow. Could you not see that I was almost equal to the other men whom I have so long admired? But now I have been cut down. I am in disgrace among my fellows. Oh, how could you do this to me?"

He was humiliated and chagrined and a drop of bitterness was in his heart, when he seemed to hear an echo from the past. Where had he heard those words before? They seemed familiar. Memory whispered:

"I'm the gardener here."

He caught his breath. Ah, that was it—the currant bush! But why should that long-forgotten incident come to him in the midst of his hour of tragedy? And memory answered with words which he himself had spoken:

"Do not cry . . . what I have done to you was necessary. . . . You were not intended for what you sought to be. . . . If I had allowed you to continue . . . you would have failed in the purpose for which I planted you and my plans for you would have been defeated. You must not weep; some day when you are richly laden with experience you will say, 'He was a wise gardener. He knew the purpose of my earth life. . . . I thank him now for what I thought was cruel.'"

His own words were the medium by which his prayer was answered. There was no bitterness in his heart as he humbly spoke again to God and said: "I know you now. *You* are the gardener, and *I* the currant bush. Help me, dear God, to endure the pruning, and to grow as you would have me grow; to take my allotted place in life and ever more to say, 'Thy will, not mine, be done.'"

Another lapse of time in our story. Forty years have passed. The former gardener and officer sits by his fireside with his wife and children and grandchildren. He tells them the story of the currant bush—his own story; and as he kneels in prayer with them, he reverently says to God, "Help us all to understand the purpose of our being, and be ever willing to submit to thy will and not insist upon our own. We remember that in another garden called Gethsemane the choicest of all thy sons was glorified by submission unto thy will." (Hugh B. Brown, *Eternal Quest,* Bookcraft, 1956, pp. 243-46.)

Acceptance of things we cannot change applies frequently to such incidents in our lives as the death of a loved one, loss of good health, loss of a limb or an organ, loss of a job or a business, and many things along these lines. These apparent tragedies are irreversible, final, and they stagger us at first. President Brown's story should help you understand that when you are greatly disappointed and your plans seem to have mired down, what really may be happening is that you are being offered a new beginning which is more in harmony with the Lord's plans. If you trust God, you will take it that way. You will not become bitter and decide that there is no plan or pattern, no use in working on the three Cs of trust. Instead, you will dig in and do the best with what lies directly before you.

The greatest poetic essay ever written, according to many of the world's greatest poets themselves, is the book of Job. Many believe Solomon wrote it before his moral decay; others credit it to Moses; still others to Baruch, or to some otherwise unscriptural writer, possibly even Job himself. Regardless of who the author was, it is a great examination of suffering caused by events outside the victim's control. It has helped millions of sufferers through the ages maintain their trust in God.

There are many things we cannot change, and still others we should not try to change even if we could. A currant bush should not try to be a poplar tree, figuratively speaking. At least that much of President Brown's analogy is useful to everyone. It refers to all our attributes that are genetic or that otherwise cannot be essentially altered—only enhanced. We should accept such things as height and general physical characteristics. No amount of stretching will make us taller; no amount of stooping will make us shorter, but only ridiculous. It will only worsen the problem, because others will perceive us as having problems—not physical but emotional problems. There are advantages in any physical characteristic. We should look for and enhance the advantages, not dwell on the disadvantages. If a person naturally has a bass voice, he shouldn't envy the tenor who gets the lead part. If a person doesn't have an outstanding voice—if the "instrument" isn't there—trying to be a soloist or an operatic star will waste a lot of time and create a lot of frustration. Some would resort to plastic surgery to alter the shape of their noses; but such extreme measures are not wise for the majority of us. Acceptance of things we cannot change is the best course, and often this shows trust in God.

Young ladies can usually create hairdos, makeup, and dress styles that will allow the natural beauty to shine through more than enough to attract the proper young men. The same principle applies to young men, but in a masculine way. Personalities can be enhanced within limits that rule out affectation and hypocrisy. These improvements should be made. They involve rules of neatness, cleanliness, and honesty inside and out. Virtue is the most beautiful attribute a person can have.

I enjoy the lines in the play "Our Town," wherein Emily and her mother are having one of those intimate mother-daughter talks. Emily is pleased that George Gibbs has noticed her, but she is concerned about her physical beauty. Emily asks her mother if she is pretty. Her mother responds, "Oh, Emily, you are pretty enough for all normal purposes."

I don't want to leave the impression that if you do everything right, the road will be easy and free from trouble and error. Your trust in God must go further than that. This life was not designed that way. If it were, I certainly would have cause to be concerned. I have had many disappointments in my life. In high school I tried out for football and basketball and was the first one cut from the teams. I tried school politics and lost every election. I didn't seem to be successful in any of the things that seemed important then, including dating. But that doesn't mean I shouldn't have tried to participate in those activities.

I wasn't valedictorian, nor was I president of any class, club, or even priesthood quorum. In the mission field I was not called to any leadership position. I had friends and enjoyed many experiences and did receive some recognition; but the things I sought after seemed to evade me. I developed something much more valuable, however. Somehow, I prayed enough to establish a close relationship with my Father in Heaven. I trusted him to know what was best for me. I didn't expect him to intervene and give me something that would lead in the wrong direction. Neither did I believe that my failures were rebukes.

After my mission I began to have some significant successes. The first was a wife who was a great source of pride. Also, my banking career went very well, and I received promotion after promotion. We had a beautiful life and a lovely family. But tragedy struck suddenly. My wife was killed in an airplane accident. That was a tremendous test of my trust in the Lord. He did come to my aid, giving the deep consolation, the acceptance and understanding that come from that divine source. Within two years, my life had begun again with another marriage to a lovely, talented, and spiritual companion who was also a great source of pride. My trust in the Lord was confirmed.

As I look back upon my life, which I have briefly outlined above, I can see how easily I could have failed to achieve the goals that are really worthwhile if I had not trusted in God when circumstances beyond my control opened new doors. My life now is in great contrast to what it was and easily may have continued to be. I was living as a banker—respected in the community, paid to live on the level of the wealthiest clients with whom I associated. Though raised on a farm, milking cows by hand, doing ordinary chores as a farm boy, I was now associating with the leaders of industry and commerce, with diplomats, generals, cabinet-level government leaders, and presidents of countries.

I was active in the Church, president of the district, but worldly things were very much on my mind. I had two boats at the yacht club; a high-performance plane hangared at the airport; three uniformed live-in servants, one to cook, one to be nursemaid to the newborn baby, and the third to clean the large and imposing home. I had a life-style equal to that of the local millionaires, and we hunted together, fished together, played polo together, skied together. Then came the tragedy of which I spoke that took the life of my companion, and suddenly none of those activities were important. Yes, I had had a lot of fun, and the memories lingered, but the one thing now of importance was the temple marriage, the certainty of the life beyond the veil, and eternity together; the spiritual things now were the *only* things. All else was temporary and fleeting—easily lost. No longer were the planes and polo ponies important.

But there was yet another factor. It was this that truly humbled me to the depths. I blamed myself for the accident. I felt the blame just as surely as did another man whom I had met who had fallen asleep while driving and had caused the death of his wife and children. I was not with my wife when the wing came off and the plane went down, but I felt that I was responsible for the circumstances. I felt that my life no longer had any value. I believed that I was of no worth at all to anyone.

Then I prayed for strength, for I needed the love of the Lord to survive; and it came. It came when I needed it most. I became filled with a certainty that I was worth something to the Lord. I felt his presence and his comfort. I felt a new security; but I was now so humbled that my only thought was *How can I serve him?* I was grateful and thankful. I felt forgiveness and love from him to a degree never before impressed upon my being. I renewed my trust in the Lord and felt that he did trust me. I knew in a different way that all mortal and temporal things are of fleeting importance. I knew also that, at times, I was subject to circumstances beyond my own control. A new, more mature humility had come to me. Now I understood what it meant to be "poor in spirit" and to "come unto him."

Consolation comes only to those who accept the will of the Lord and who come to see his purposes through that which causes the sorrow. The Comforter is available to us; and if the Lord needs to bring us down through humbling experiences, so be it.

To accept with serenity and trust the things we cannot change is to trust in the wisdom of the Lord.

I trusted in the Lord, I remarried, and a few years later I was called to serve as president of one of the Mexican missions. Another major test came into my life just before the end of that mission. I was asked to fly to Salt Lake City to be interviewed by one of the leaders of the Church. This brother had asked me some months earlier if I was interested in Church employment, but I had quickly turned down that initiative because I didn't feel we could live on the salary. This second time the offer was made, again at the same salary, but with the suggestion that I pray about it. It was made clear that this was not a call and that there was no tenure or job security.

My wife and I fasted and prayed and received the unmistakable impression that we should leave the security and high salary of the banking career, with all its prestige and fringe benefits, and accept the Church position. We didn't know why. We simply knew that this was a test we must pass. Our only thought was this: *The Lord seems to want us in Salt Lake City. We know it is a salaried job, but it seems to be the will of the Lord. We will trust in him.*

Just as we had always trusted in the Lord's wisdom and hidden plan, we now proceeded to trust the answer to our prayers and left what we believed to be a sure and prosperous career for that of a salaried servant of the Church in the Purchasing Department. This experience proved to be a helpful preparation for a subsequent call to the First Quorum of the Seventy. Of course, our faith was well founded, and we haven't suffered. We have been frustrated from time to time, but never have we had anything but certainty in trusting the Lord. We have never doubted the inspiration nor the prompting of the Spirit. And we now have seen much of what he planned for our lives.

Character That Merits Trust

I came to feel, through years of experience as a loan officer, that a person can be trusted if he lives up to his own code. Of course, that code had to be an acceptable standard for the bank's purpose, which was the recovery of the amount loaned and the interest—on time. This matter of being true to one's code is very important. Without it, there is a lack of unity and peace within the soul. President David O. McKay illustrated this with a story many years ago in a general conference:

The strength and growth of character depends upon a life consistent with that testimony; and it takes character to live in harmony with a man's ideals, or at least to strive to live in harmony with them.

I can illustrate what I mean by relating an incident concerning two of our boys at college. They had been taught as you boys and I have been taught, that next to life itself, we should cherish chastity.

One of these boys noticed that there was a laxity among his non-member classmates, and after a few months at college, he partook of a different spirit from the one he had in his home, and one night he said to his companion, who was older than he, "I am going out tonight with those fellows."

"Well, you'd better not," said his companion.

"Oh," he said, "I do not know! Those fellows have a good time, take their wine, have their cigarets and their cigars, they enjoy themselves; and here we are restrained. They get their lessons; they are doing just as well in college as we are; and I am going out with them. I am not so sure that our ideals are necessary, anyhow."

The older one walked up, put his hand on his companion's shoulder, and said, "Those boys may be getting along all right in school; they may do these things to which you refer with impunity; but you can't."

"Why?"

"Because you know better. And *once you break through that ideal, your character is broken.*"

It was the best lesson he learned in college, and I am very glad that he learned it and lived it. (*Conference Report*, October 1918, pp. 137-38.)

Character has been defined as an intangible sum of personal attributes. These attributes are revealed in how we live our daily lives. We can measure them ourselves, and inevitably they are measured by others. What we say and do to others tells much more about our character than what others may say about us. How we talk, act, and think is governed by character. How others perceive our words and actions and talk about them is our reputation. Character and reputation often are confused. A reputation is only the opinion held by others about us. It may be better or worse than our character. Character is an inward thing. Only the Lord can truly and impartially weigh all the factors and come up with a true total. Mortals can make only partial judgments based on such things as business or professional conduct; prompt payment of obligations; speculative tendencies; respect for the rights of others; personal habits, including drinking and gambling; and so forth. Actually a person may have a good reputation simply because he has never been pressed by adversity or great temptation. This probably is what Solomon had in mind when he said, "All things have I seen in the days of my vanity: there is a just man that perisheth in his righteousness, and there is a wicked man that prolongeth his life in his wickedness." (Ecclesiastes 7:15.) Character, even if defined, cannot be measured or appraised exactly, nor always fairly, even by intimate associates.

One of my dear wife's favorite quotations on character goes like this: "Character is the ability to follow through with resolutions long after the mood in which they were made has passed." She has often used this when speaking to missionaries. In my notes I have another quotation which says, "What a man continually thinks about determines his actions in times of opportunity or stress. A man's reaction to his appetites and impulses when they are aroused gives the measure of that man's character. Character seems to have a great deal to do with the power of a person to govern his own actions or to yield in servility to inside or outside forces."

A banker has some difficulty when evaluating the character of a client. The usual manner is to gather references from such sources as other banks, credit information agencies, competitors, sources who also extend credit to the client (such as suppliers), and then to form a composite picture from this complex medley of personal history, traits, and qualities. The banker is really trying to identify the moral risk. Will the client really be honest and use the funds for the purpose approved, or will he take the money and move to the Bahamas or Brazil? Will the client do everything in his power to repay the loan, regardless of the personal sacrifice, or will he walk away from the obligation if struck with disaster, bad luck, or misfortune? The banker wants to uncover the client's past record of intentions and willingness to comply so that he can apply what he discovers to unknown future events. The banker looks at the worst possible scenario—inflation, high interest rates, new competition, and all other factors of the economic environment, both national and international—and ponders the character of his client when under stress. But as objective as he tries to be, he always has to fall back on his own judgment to some extent.

Should the banker judge and measure the client by his own standards, or can the client have a different set of standards and still be considered morally sound for banking purposes? If in a banker's opinion good character includes active church membership, he will get a negative opinion when the credit applicant is not active in a church. The banker may be a foe of alcohol and tobacco and have a very negative opinion of the client who is a social drinker and a puffer of smoke; but does that really mean that the client would not live up to his financial obligations?

As I indicated earlier, my way out of this dilemma, based on years of experience as a loan officer, was to trust a person if he lived up to his own code.

Whether we like it or not, people will tend to brand us as hypocrites and will not trust us if we are not true to our own codes. Many scriptures say or imply that God judges us by the laws we have. That is, his trust depends on how well we live up to the codes we have developed. We are constantly developing our own codes to live by in the sum of our daily actions. In other words, we carve out our own destiny, or as Harry Emerson Fosdick put it, "Every man's fate is himself." Every small act, good or bad, leaves its mark and thereby shapes habit and character.

We need not be discouraged by this fact, for let me remind you that the atonement of Christ can wipe away all sins and relieve us from the punishment of the great and last day if we repent and struggle constantly for perfection. But the point I am making is that sin tends to beget sin, and righteousness tends to beget righteousness. And even though guilt can be swept away, the habit of sin can keep coming back to haunt us throughout our mortal lives. The roots are down there in the nerve cells and fibers. And even when God has forgiven us, sometimes the world has not. Hence it is not easy to rebuild trust when it has been lost.

Character may well be the principal attribute we are able to take with us into the next life. We don't know in detail what we accomplished in the premortal life; but we know that we were divided into two main groups: those who were faithful enough to be born and receive a body and those who were not allowed to have bodies because they followed Satan and were cast out. Among those who come here and receive bodies there is a wide variety of gifts, talents, and opportunities. Some are born into the lineage of Israel, while others are born into situations wherein they will never hear the gospel in this life. Some circumstances can be explained only by concluding that they are a result of diligence in heaven before birth. I refer primarily to the "noble and great ones" whom God makes his rulers. (See Abraham 3:22-28; Jeremiah 1:5.) These are the ones who can be trusted. No doubt this could refer to many of the Saints and to many others outside of the Church who have special missions. So, also, we take into the postmortal spirit world those attributes of the spirit which we have developed here in perfecting our strength of character. I rejoice in the philosophy that one of the main things we can take home to our Heavenly Father is that which we call a noble character. We are wise when we use the short years of this probation to improve that which we will take back to our Maker. The character we have molded will be of the greatest importance when we are weighed in the balance. The essence of this character is trustworthiness. The Lord will measure our trustworthiness by the self-discipline we have achieved. An old Hindu proverb says, "There is nothing noble in being superior to some other person—true nobility [true character] is in being superior to your own previous self."

Self-discipline and self-control are never easy to achieve. One philosopher said, "I have more trouble with myself than with any other man I have ever met." The great test of character is how a person takes charge of his own life in seeking to achieve higher goals. No one need stay the way he is now. The glory comes from the height of the goals which are set and the progress made toward those goals in relation to one's own previous goals and previous progress. So that we won't get discouraged by setting impossible short-range goals, we must use wisdom in determining how rapidly we try to improve. We can, however, control short-range results much more than we sometimes realize. Our destinies are not reached through luck or chance. They really are the result of our own deeds—and these deeds are the result of our thoughts.

The idea that there is a cause-effect relationship at work in our lives is fortified by Doctrine and Covenants 130:20-21:

> There is a law, irrevocably decreed in heaven before the foundations of this world, upon which all blessings are predicated—
> And when we obtain any blessing from God, it is by obedience to that law upon which it is predicated.

Attaining good character (trustworthiness) is a thought process, a matter of attitudes. This is illustrated by James Allen in a book he wrote called *As a Man Thinketh*. The heart of the book is reflected in a couple of pages wherein he declares that one's character is the complete sum of one's thoughts and then tells why:

> A man is literally *what he thinks*, his character being the complete sum of all his thoughts.
> As the plant springs from, and could not be without, the seed, so every act of a man springs from the hidden seeds of thought, and could not have appeared without them. . . .
> Act is the blossom of thought, and joy and suffering are its fruits; thus does a man garner in the sweet and bitter fruitage of his own husbandry. . . .
> A man's mind may be likened to a garden, which may be intelligently cultivated or allowed to run wild; but whether cultivated or neglected, it must, and will *bring forth*. If no useful seeds are *put* into it, then an abundance of useless weed seeds will *fall* therein, and will continue to produce their kind.
> Just as a gardener cultivates his plot, keeping it free from weeds, and growing the flowers and fruits which he requires, so may a man tend the garden of his mind, weeding out all the wrong, useless, and impure thoughts, and cultivating toward perfection the flowers and fruits of right, useful, and pure thoughts. By pursuing this process, a man sooner or

later discovers that he is the master gardener of his soul, the director of his life. He also reveals, within himself, the laws of thought, and understands, with ever-increasing accuracy, how the thought forces and mind elements operate in the shaping of his character, circumstances, and destiny. . . .

Man is buffeted by circumstances so long as he believes himself to be the creature of outside conditions, but when he realizes that he is a creative power, and that he may command the hidden soil and seeds of his being out of which circumstances grow, he then becomes the rightful master of himself. . . .

. . . Good thoughts bear good fruit, bad thoughts bad fruit.

. . . [A man] will find that as he alters his thoughts toward things, and other people, things and other people will alter toward him. . . .

Let a man radically alter his thoughts, and he will be astonished at the rapid transformation it will effect in the material conditions of his life.

Men do not attract that which they *want,* but that which they *are.* . . . The "divinity that shapes our ends" is in ourselves; it is our very self. . . . All that a man achieves or fails to achieve is the direct result of his own thoughts. . . . A man can only rise, conquer, and achieve by lifting up his thoughts. He can only remain weak, and abject, and miserable by refusing to lift up his thoughts. . . .

A man should conceive of a legitimate purpose in his heart, and set out to accomplish it. He should make this purpose the centralising point of his thoughts . . . he should steadily focus his thought forces upon the object which he has set before him. He should make this purpose his supreme duty, and should devote himself to its attainment, not allowing his thoughts to wander away into ephemeral fancies, longings, and imaginings. This is the royal road to self-control and true concentration of thought. Even if he fails again and again to accomplish his purpose (as he necessarily must until weakness is overcome), the *strength of character gained* will be the measure of his true success, and this will form a new starting point for future power and triumph.

. . . Into your hands will be placed the exact results of your own thoughts; you will receive that which you earn; no more, no less. Whatever your present environment may be, you will fall, remain, or rise with your thoughts, your Vision, your Ideal. You will become as small as your controlling desire; as great as your dominant aspiration. . . .

The thoughtless, the ignorant, and the indolent, seeing only the apparent effects of things and not the things themselves, talk of luck, of fortune, and chance. Seeing a man grow rich, they say, "How lucky he is!" Observing another become intellectual, they exclaim, "How highly favored he is!" And noting the saintly character and wide influence of another, they remark, "How chance aids him at every turn!" They do not see the trials and failures and struggles which these men have voluntarily encountered in order to gain their experience; have no knowledge of the sacrifices they have made, of the undaunted efforts they have put forth, of the faith they have exercised, that they might overcome the apparently insurmountable, and realise the Vision of their heart. They do not know the darkness and the heartaches; they only see the light and joy, and call it "luck"; do not see the long and arduous journey, but only behold the pleasant goal, and call it "good fortune"; do not understand the process, but only perceive the results and call it "chance."

In all human affairs there are *efforts,* and there are *results,* and the strength of effort is the measure of the result. Chance is not. "Gifts," powers, material, intellectual, and spiritual possessions are the fruits of effort; they are thoughts completed, objects accomplished, visions realised.

The Vision that you glorify in your mind, the Ideal that you enthrone in your heart—this you will build your life by, this you will become.

It is surely true, as someone has said, that "The destiny of nations is determined by the thoughts of its youth!" We can preserve only what is treasured in their hearts. They will destroy all the rest. This gives greater meaning to Solomon's counsel: "Train up a child in the way he should go: and when he is old, he will not depart from it." (Proverbs 22:6.)

Character is built in the schools, on the playing fields, in the churches, in service activities; and, more than in any other place, character is built in the home. So I wish to direct some remarks at parents in the hope the remarks will encourage someone to try to give every child a good start in life.

The home, especially if there are loving parents, is the most fertile field for the growth of character. The home is the best place to teach self-restraint, self-control, respect for the rights of others, delight in the soft tones of peace and order, and admiration for the beauty of good music and art. Parents may think they are making little progress in achieving those lofty goals as permanent and deeply embedded characteristics in their children; nevertheless, sometimes we see young missionaries who, while at home they were still rebelling against making beds and being nice to little brothers and sisters, on their mission make an about-face. There they begin to appreciate and to follow what was taught in the home. Parents can be proud of their efforts. The years of training pay off. Young students at college and young missionaries frequently say, "I'm glad my parents taught me what they did." Or they may say, "Oh, I wish my parents had been even more strict!"

Children profit by understanding that there are bounds beyond which they cannot pass with safety. I still remember when it suddenly dawned upon me as a young man that what my parents warned against was likely to happen. Even if it didn't happen every time, it was surely going to happen sometime; and when it did, I would regret not having obeyed their counsel. Young people tend to be short-sighted; and the worst part is that they tend to be shortsighted just when they need most the long view that their parents can see. Parents will be wise if they teach their children to respect the elderly—especially when they are aunts, uncles, grandparents, Church leaders and teachers. Yes, inevitably there will be some trusted adult who will be found guilty of hypocrisy—someone who professes one standard and lives another. But parents can use that situation as an object lesson to show the importance of righteousness and to prove the value and power of the teachings of the Church. This kind of tragedy can even be used as an example of how not to fall to Satan.

The home is the best place to teach consideration for the rights of others. From a very early age, children should respect each other's closets, drawers, rooms, toys, journals, tools, and so forth. This reinforces the value of honesty. Home conversations should praise the correct acts and attitudes while finding an appropriate way to correct or punish offenders. A great Mexican patriot-president once said, "Respect for the rights of others is peace." If peace is not present in a home, perhaps it is because not every member of the family is yet respecting, in every sense, the rights of every other family member. Some parents are guilty of failure to appreciate and respect the inherent individual rights of their children. And, of course, some children may not be acting with sufficient self-control to deserve the rights for which they ask. How can a parent give children the right to set the place they will go to and the hour they will come home from dates if the children have not demonstrated the good judgment, the wisdom, and the character to stay within that which is safe?

The home can contribute to character growth by creating an environment that will cause children to feel that home is a place where confidence and consolation are exchanged. Home should be a place where we can go to recuperate from the battles of the world. Some battles produce real wounds on the outside of the body, and home is where the little boy or girl gets the disinfectant, bandages, and tender loving care to help wipe away the tears and hurts. Home also can be the place to receive the peace, understanding, and consolation we need to face the quiet, silent inner battles of disappointment, discouragement, unrequited love, misunderstandings, failures (being cut from the team, dropping below the acceptable grade-point average, having no date to the prom), and all the things that happen in all young lives. Character is built in properly meeting these big tragedies of today that will be small incidents a few years hence. Home can be the training ground for greater battles and challenges to come.

A good goal for parents to set is to make the home a place where all family members can find seclusion and rest from the worries and perplexities of life. All need peace and rest of spirit just as they need peace and rest of body. It helps if the home has that degree of orderliness and beauty that is restful to both body and spirit. It can be done without carpets, expensive artwork, and expansive gardens with statues in artistic places. If it is clean, neat, pleasant, if it has things in place and has a flower here, a picture on a wall there, if it has scriptures and Church magazines available—if it contains these modest amenities the home can give peace to the spirit and orderliness to the eye. Civilization depends upon the home. Without proper homes and families, domestic virtue disappears and law and order break down.

Kindness to animals, to children, to invalids, to the aged, to mankind in general is a beloved character quality. Kindness is honored and respected in womanhood. Women seem to come by it naturally, as do the most masculine of men. You can find evidence of this in the histories of such manly characters as our prophets. Joseph Smith, David O. McKay and Spencer W. Kimball are notable examples of the most manly of men who have said much about kindness to the weak, to the feeble, and also to animals. The home is the best place to teach these qualities of kindness. Parents should not only teach kindness in family home evenings, but also should look for teaching moments that arise constantly in the home.

Reverence for sacred things is a great quality of character. It should not matter whether the subject is sacred to the person himself. If it is sacred to anyone—be it a statue of Buddha, a crucifix, the Virgin Mary—it should be highly respected by the rest of us. A person of good character instinctively respects the sacred things of other religions and of his own. He also treats womanhood and sex with high respect and chivalry.

A man of character honors his country, its flag, and its national anthem. And he doesn't speak lightly of patriotism. I hold in contempt those writers who would look for flaws in their country's heroes. Certainly every man is human, with normal frailties; but should we flaunt those weaknesses in such a way as to diminish the love and respect we have for their finest hours in the service of their native lands? Certainly not. And this, again, is something that parents should teach children at an early age.

Wise parents do not overlook what they can do in the home to instill in children an awareness of and an appreciation for the sacred nature of fatherhood and motherhood. Chastity can best be taught by parents who express and show love for the child and love for each other. Different aspects of sex are wisely taught at different times or stages of the life of the young person. The parent should seek some ideas and guidance on the subject from appropriate authors and Church leaders; and actual conversation on these sacred subjects should occur between parent and child. To avoid such vital conversations may weaken the respect and honor the child will give this sacred subject. No amount of expertise and teaching ability can compensate for the loving authority of the parent. Virtue and chastity give youthful men their vigor, strength, and stamina, and then later their virility in marriage and manhood. Chastity is the crown of beauty that leads girls to queenly presence in this life and in the life to come. The blessings received by those of high moral character are really worth the effort it takes to resist all the temptations of Satan, all the arguments of the worldly wise, and all the justifications of the already sinful.

Perhaps my greatest desire is to have each reader feel encouraged with the prospect of constant improvement, not discouraged at his present state of development. There is a spiral shell, a pearly nautilus, formed by a small mollusk. As the mollusk grows larger and larger, it moves on in gradually enlarging compartments or chambers which have a fascinating beauty. Dr. Oliver Wendell Holmes—not the Supreme Court Justice, but his father—observing this lovely and unique shell, wrote a poetic analogy about humans trying to move onward and upward in growing and expanding spirals, constantly creating new mansions. He felt that each man is responsible for being the architect of his own character. Note especially the poem's most famous line: "Build thee more stately mansions, O my soul."

The Chambered Nautilus

This is the ship of pearl, which, poets feign,
    Sails the unshadowed main—
    The venturous bark that flings
On the sweet summer wind its purpled wings
In gulfs enchanted, where the Siren sings,
    And coral reefs lie bare,
Where the cold sea-maids rise to sun their streaming hair.

Its webs of living gauze no more unfurl;
    Wrecked is the ship of pearl!
    And every chambered cell,
Where its dim dreaming life was wont to dwell,
As the frail tenant shaped his growing shell,
    Before thee lies revealed—
Its irised ceiling rent, its sunless crypt unsealed!

Year after year beheld the silent toil
    That spread his lustrous coil;
    Still, as the spiral grew,
He left the past year's dwelling for the new,
Stole with soft step its shining archway through,
    Built up its idle door,
Stretched in his last-found home, and knew the old no more.

Thanks for the heavenly message brought by thee,
    Child of the wandering sea,
    Cast from her lap, forlorn!
From thy dead lips a clearer note is born
Than ever Triton blew from wreathed horn!
    While on mine ear it rings,
Through the deep caves of thought I hear a voice that sings:

Build thee more stately mansions, O my soul,
    As the swift seasons roll!
    Leave thy low-vaulted past!
Let each new temple, nobler than the last,
Shut thee from heaven with a dome more vast,
    Till thou at length art free,
Leaving thine outgrown shell by life's unresting sea!

(*The New Pocket Anthology of American Verse*, Oscar Williams, ed., Washington Square Press, Inc., [New York: 1955], pp. 229-30.)

Trustworthy Capacity

If you really believe that the Church is the kingdom of God and that the Lord really needs you—not someone else, but *you*—what will you do? Will you not prepare as best you can within the limits of the gifts and talents the Lord has given you? And are not these gifts and talents usually very many? They do not represent capacity while lying dormant. They represent capacity when they have been developed to the point that they can be used.

Let me return to the banking analogy for perspective. Capacity to a banker may mean nothing more or less than the ability to pay the dollar obligation when it comes due. In a broader sense, capacity is a measure of the many different sources to which the client can go for funds to make repayment. Information related to an individual's capacity to pay is often summarized under such headings as salary, employment, job security and stability, outside income, monies soon to be collected, relative pressure from other obligations, and so on.

In analyzing a credit request from a company, a banker will also measure the capacity of the company to meet its short-term and long-term obligations against income, profits, cash flow, and so forth. The loan officer tries to form a composite picture in his mind and on paper of all the factors involved, factors such as management capacity, technical capacity to meet the sales estimates and production goals, capacity to raise new capital, and capacity to develop new products to meet the competition. One way of stating the point of view of the banker is to say that he evaluates the capacity of the firm or individual to operate on a sound and profitable business basis during the duration of the loan. Other intangibles are included in this, such as resourcefulness, imagination, creativity, all demonstrated over a period of time so that they have instilled in the banker a confidence and trust in the person's or the firm's capacity.

When a person develops capacity, he or she is demonstrating trust —trust in the general providence of the Lord, and trust that someone will appreciate that developed capacity and offer employment or the use of capital (money that has been saved) to start a business. The Lord has created a bounteous world that is governed by laws we commonly call "nature." Nature is bounteous and helpful within the laws the Lord has set. And everybody who has capital wants to use it to better or to enrich himself. Hence, those with capital are anxiously looking for people of ability to employ or to set up in business. If it looks otherwise to you, that is only because you have not come to fully appreciate how scarce a "commodity" is well-developed capacity.

Now, if the reader will imagine that he is a stake president (or she is a stake Relief Society president) and that all those over whom he presides recognize that they owe great sums to the kingdom, he will see that this will clarify the daily task of looking for capacity to "pay" in the kingdom. To put it another way, if the reader will again assume his own role of debtor—for we all are in the debt of the Lord—he will see more clearly what must be done to prepare to serve, or in other words, to obtain the capacity to serve.

Again, when a person develops the capacity to serve in the king-dom—and generally that means developing the same capacity that one develops to make a living or to flourish in business—he is demonstrating trust in Heavenly Father and his servants who are in charge of Heavenly Father's business here upon the earth. (Remember Luke 2:49: "I must be about my Father's business.") He is saying, "I trust that Heavenly Father wants me to have a mansion in his house. I trust that he will provide it if I work for it. I trust he will provide the grace to take care of what I cannot take care of myself. My work will be worthwhile. It will not be wasted. I can trust my Heavenly Father. He will find that he can trust me. I will show my gratitude for the talents and gifts he has given me by developing them. In this way he can give me tasks to do that will help me while I am helping him." We should be anxiously engaged in the good cause of building up the kingdom, including the temporal work that makes it possible to do the kingdom work. There is a good scripture about that:

> For behold, it is not meet that I should command in all things; for he that is compelled in all things, the same is a slothful and not a wise servant; wherefore he receiveth no reward.
>
> Verily I say, men should be anxiously engaged in a good cause, and do many things of their own free will, and bring to pass much righteousness;
>
> For the power is in them, wherein they are agents unto themselves. And inasmuch as men do good they shall in nowise lose their reward.
>
> But he that doeth not anything until he is commanded, and receiveth a commandment with doubtful heart, and keepeth it with slothfulness, the same is damned. (D&C 58:26-29.)

Some excuse their indecision by saying, "Oh, but I do not covet wealth or position." They are confused. It is coveting to desire or to plan to get someone else's wife, husband, or wealth; but it is not coveting to prepare and to seek to get your own. Remember how wealthy and famous was Job, one of the most perfect men who ever lived. And, after the Lord tested Job, he doubled what he had had before.

We cannot double our God-given capacity without work. Work is the essence of capacity. Our capacity is what we can do, how well we can do it, how willing we are to do it, and how well all that fits with what we think we want to do. And all of that involves work.

You might say that there are natural or latent gifts and talents in each of us. They are part of the basis for capacity. But they are almost useless without the work that develops them and the later work that capitalizes on them. Dreams may be the stuff life is made of, but only if at least twenty hours of work follow every one of the dreams. So, if I were to place a priority on the characteristic of capacity for both spiritual and worldly usefulness, it would be the capacity for plain, old-fashioned hard work. The "gospel of work" it is sometimes called. "By the sweat of thy brow," a saying as old as the human race, is an integral part of this life as the Lord designed it. Any effort to avoid work is doomed to failure and disappointment; and any effort to ennoble, elevate, and honor it is worthy of our attention.

One of the bright stars in Great Britain's shining galaxy of writers, Thomas Carlyle, gave us this in one of his essays:

> There is a perennial nobleness, and even sacredness, in work. Were he ever so benighted, forgetful of his high calling, there is always hope in a man that actually and earnestly works. In idleness alone is there perpetual despair.
>
> The latest gospel in this world is, "Know thy work and do it." It has been written, "An endless significance lies in work." A man perfects himself by working. Foul jungles are cleared away, fair seed fields rise instead, and stately cities. . . .
>
> Blessed is he who has found his work: let him ask no other blessedness. He has a work, a life-purpose: he has found it and will follow it. . . . Labor is life. (*Past and Present.*)

Carlyle is really saying that we must get our happiness out of our work or we will never know what real happiness is. I am always impressed with genius in its many manifestations, but I am even more impressed by those who consistently work harder than those about them. I love Henry Van Dyke's poem on work:

> Let me but do my work from day to day,
>   In field or forest, at the desk or loom,
>   In roaring market-place or tranquil room;
> Let me but find it in my heart to say,
> When vagrant wishes beckon me astray,
>   "This is my work; my blessing, not my doom;
>   Of all who live, I am the one by whom
> This work can best be done in the right way."
> Then shall I see it not too great, nor small,
>   To suit my spirit and to prove my powers;
>   Then shall I cheerful greet the laboring hours,
> And cheerful turn, when the long shadows fall
> At eventide, to play and love and rest,
>   Because I know for me my work is best.

You cannot separate capacity from work—love of work, untiring work, work till the job is done, work while the sun shines, noble work, assigned work, necessary work. Each of us should ask these questions: Does the Lord know how hard I am willing to work? Have I proved my work capacity to him so that he can trust me? Does my priesthood leader know of my willingness to work? Preparation for service and attempts to increase capacity will involve work. Learning to love work must be at least half the battle.

Successful work requires matching our individual gifts to the opportunities that life presents us. We all have special gifts. These special gifts do not come totally developed. They are greater in some than others. Some have an easier time developing them than others do. But all have to work. And the general opportunities—such as parenthood, genealogical work, home teaching, visiting teaching, and the rest of the daily and compassionate service—are one long and vast school ground of work. The harder we work at them, the more we come to love them and to see that they are the very foundation of true Christianity.

There are some specially choice passages of scripture that lay the foundation of creating the capacity for the general work of the kingdom that the Lord entrusts to our care. One of these is the Sermon on the Mount. You might call it the very foundation of true Christian conduct. It also is the finishing school, because no mortal has ever plumbed its full depths. I commend to you the Nephite version (3 Nephi 12, 13, 14) because it brings the Bible version up to date for all members after the Law of Moses was fulfilled. There is no substitute for reading and pondering these verses yourself. However, let me list a few of the principles Jesus taught in that sermon:

1. All the blessings of the kingdom are granted only if we "come unto" Christ.

2. If we prepare to accept twice as much abuse as we are ever likely to have to accept, we will always be in charge of our feelings and attitudes.

3. Even though we may have to wait sometimes, we receive pretty much the same as we give.

4. The thought precedes the deed. If we keep our minds pure, we will avoid sin.

5. We should not teach sacred things to those who are not ready to hear them and who will trample them into the mire.

6. It is the General Authorities who are to take no thought for the morrow. We may be asked by them to take thought of a whole year of tomorrows.

7. We have to be singleminded in our devotion to the kingdom. We cannot serve two masters. We cannot love the world and the kingdom at the same time.

8. We should not try to perfect others until we are perfect.

9. God will answer our prayers.

10. We should do unto others as we would have others do unto us.

11. Many follow error. Few follow truth.

12. Beware of false prophets. We can know them by their fruits.

13. Doing the will of the Father, not the performing of miracles, is the supreme measure of sainthood.

14. We can become perfect as the Father and the Son are perfect.

Once we have laid the foundation of Christian conduct as described in the Sermon on the Mount, we must cultivate the latent capacity God has built into us in the form of spiritual gifts. In Doctrine and Covenants 46:10-33 we can review the meaning of these gifts of the Spirit. Many readings and prayerful ponderings will help us understand our own gifts so that we can get direction for specialization in our preparations to serve. (The Topical Guide and the Index in the new standard works will lead us to many other passages for further study.) Note that section 46 makes it clear that if we are born again, we are guaranteed one or the other of two basic gifts: to know by the power of the Holy Ghost that Jesus is the Christ, or to have faith through the Holy Ghost in the testimony of those who do know. In addition to that, the Holy Ghost may grant additional gifts as he pleases. Thus the whole Church can be edified by all of the gifts of the Spirit. Also note that we are encouraged to seek the best gifts.

While we should seek the best gifts, one of the chief gifts is the spirit of service. This is very important to our developing trustworthy capacity in the kingdom. I find it interesting that Job, whom God called perfect even before his great trial, based his whole defense on the fact that his mind was pure and his life was filled with charitable service. (See Job 29-31, especially 31:1-12.) That is what Doctrine and Covenants, section 121, tells us is the key to obtaining confidence in the presence of the Lord: bowels filled with charity—even charity for the Church, "the household of faith"—and a mind divested of all evil thoughts. (Read especially verses 34-36.)

All these scriptures teach us the importance of enlarging our individual capacities. Wise young people will seek an exacting career requiring much training and education; for the temporal skills go hand in hand with the spiritual skills. Those who have the courage and fortitude to prepare for the most difficult careers will find that they also will be of greater service to the Church. A former bishop of a

Brigham Young University ward remarked that as a matter of principle he always sought for ward clerks and assistant ward clerks from among those students who were in the hardest types of career training. They never failed him; and the stake leaders continuously called people out of his clerical staff to fill important stake positions. These people ended up serving as bishops' counselors, stake high councilors, stake clerks, and so forth. They had the right skills and work habits. Their outstanding performance as ward clerks was soon noticed.

Consider these maxims from the book of Proverbs:

> He becometh poor that dealeth with a slack hand: but the hand of the diligent maketh rich.
> He that gathereth in summer is a wise son: but he that sleepeth in harvest is a son that causeth shame. (10:4-5.)
> The soul of the sluggard desireth, and hath nothing: but the soul of the diligent shall be made fat. (13:4.)
> He also that is slothful in his work is brother to him that is a great waster. (18:9.)
> Even a child is known by his doings, whether his work be pure, and whether it be right. (20:11.)

If we are going to be competent stewards in the kingdom—stewards who can manage growth as opposed to stewards of stagnation, stewards who can be profitable servants of the Lord and who can double the assets entrusted to them—we need to learn practical and proven management skills. It has been said with some truth that we need more of Church skills in business and more of business skills in the Church. In business we speak of people-management skills; money-management skills; management by exception; theory X and theory Y of management; management by goals; personalized approaches, such as Maslow's technique or those described in Peter Drucker's books (time management, priority management); and so on. In the Church we speak of the Savior's approach: He who would be greatest must learn to be the least and serve those he leads, even to the point at which, figuratively speaking, he emulates the Savior's act of washing the feet of his Apostles. Forevermore such leaders will be humble servants of the Saints rather than autocratic, dictatorial, domineering leaders. The Prophet Joseph had a singular management philosophy: "I teach them correct principles, and they govern themselves." One modern wag, somewhat frustrated because the people didn't seem to respond to that formula, decided that what the Prophet really meant to say was, "I teach them correct principles, and teach them, and teach them, and teach them, and *then* they begin to govern themselves."

Say what you will, it is true that if you have the capacity to govern yourself in patience and charity, you are going to be trusted with a lot of work all the days of your life.

CHAPTER SIX

Spiritual Capital

Capital is the third quality or aspect of our lives that is weighed by the Lord, by the earthly stewards of his kingdom, and by the stewards of "the mammon of unrighteousness," as Jesus put it. (See Luke 16:9-12.) The first quality was character, or that which is epitomized by Psalm 15:4: "He that sweareth to his own hurt, and changeth not." The second was capacity, which is characterized by what we can do, how well we can do it, how willing we are to do it, and how well that all fits with what we think we want to do. We now look at our capital, which in a spiritual sense could be described as that which we have stored up in heaven where moth and rust do not corrupt and thieves cannot break in. (See Matthew 6:19-21.)

Worldly capital includes such things as money, stocks, bonds, real estate, inventory items, raw materials, accounts receivable, and all sorts of other valuables. But spiritual capital, more than anything else, is to be found in the richness of human and divine relationships that have been properly formed and properly fostered. In the case of a Moses or a Joseph Smith, God takes some of the initiative in establishing that relationship. But most of us come to the relationships of the kingdom through the prophets, the stake leaders, the ward leaders, and other servants of the Lord. So if we wish to be friends of God, we need to learn to store up the spiritual capital of loyalty to the Church and its leaders.

One can come to the Lord and be his friend only through the servants of the Lord. The Lord designates who his servants are: He appoints them. And then he is loyal to them. He sustains them. Otherwise, his house would be a house of confusion. The friends of God's servants are the friends of God. (See D&C 84:35-38, 51-58, 77; 112:20; Matthew 10:40-42.) And conversely, by implication, the enemies of God's servants are the enemies of God. All the money in the world is not equal to the friendship of God if you are seeking the treasures that do not corrupt and never rust.

It is very difficult for some people to trust another human being, who has mortal shortcomings, as an authorized spokesman for the Lord. This resistance is vividly described in the parable of Lazarus and the rich man. The beggar, Lazarus, upon dying, went to Abraham's bosom; but the rich man, when his spirit departed, went to torment. Ultimately the departed rich man begged that Lazarus be sent to his brothers so that they might escape a fate similar to his. He was told that the brothers already had Moses and the prophets. He responded that he felt they would be more likely to listen to one who came from the dead; in fact, he was *sure* that they would listen to a messenger sent from the dead. (See Luke 16:19-31 for the whole story.) This is a very common attitude, incidentally. In fact, it has been an almost universal attitude from very early times. Members of the family of Moses, whom most consider the greatest prophet (not counting Jesus, who is a God), rebelled against him. (See Numbers 12.) And the whole nation of Israel repeatedly rebelled against him in spite of a steady stream of miracles and stern chastening from the Lord.

The rich man in the parable could not quite believe a mortal would be as convincing as one returned from the dead. Yet in this parable the Savior is telling us that our prophets are to be listened to just as much as if they were heavenly messengers. In fact, the Savior points out in this story that if a person will not accept a living prophet, he would not accept one coming from the dead either. Such is human nature.

Most people have been more willing to accept dead prophets than living prophets. It was much easier for the Jews of Jesus' day to honor those Old Testament prophets of several thousand years before than it was to honor Jesus and Paul, for example. And it is very easy for Christians in general to accept Peter and Paul but not to accept Joseph Smith. We can see the dead prophets in our minds as being much higher than mere mortals. We magnify them to the point of perfection in the flesh and overlook their weaknesses. We are certain that had we lived at the time of Noah, we would not have been one of those who rejected him; but rather we would have been right there beside Noah and his sons, hammering in the planks on the ark and gathering in the pairs of animals before the rain started.

"Yes, sir," we say. "We love the prophets, and we would not have rejected them had we lived back in their time." We are all certain in our minds that we would have followed Moses into the desert without murmuring; and we would not have participated in melting the gold to cast the golden calf. "No, sir, not us. We would have been the very faithful ones. And when Brigham Young was ready to move west, we would not have stayed behind, nor would we have voted in favor of going on to California."

It is so very easy to say how righteous we would have been had we lived two thousand years ago or one hundred years ago. We would not have denied knowing Jesus as Peter did. We would not have insisted on seeing the resurrected Lord as a prerequisite to belief as Thomas did. Had we lived then, we would have seen no defect at all in the prophets nor in the Savior, and we would have had no doubts. Therefore our own conduct would have been faultless.

Of course, the above may not apply to the reader. I have said it that way to make a point: The world in general has felt that way, but not the faithful Saints. They have accepted the prophets. Probably no one is perfect in his acceptance of the prophets. But in general the active, tithed Saints accept and follow the prophets. And they would have if they had lived in the earlier times. (See Matthew 23:29-33 and Acts 7:51-53. As you read these passages bear in mind that there was the faithful minority as well as the faithless majority.) You can be very sure that your acceptance of Moses, if you had lived then, would have been neither greater nor less than your present acceptance of the living prophet at the head of The Church of Jesus Christ of Latter-day Saints. If you objected to the change in policy about who can hold the priesthood in our day, you, like Miriam, would have objected to Moses having an Ethiopian wife. And, like her, you would have said, "Who is Moses that he should have a monopoly on these decisions about where the Church should stand?"

The problem with some occurs when they face a living prophet in our own time, one who dresses in just about the way we do; one who may have been quite "mortal" at some time—had something to do with an enterprise that failed, or supported a certain program that was afterwards discontinued because it didn't work as anticipated, or one who has a child or a grandchild who does not follow the example and teachings of his illustrious parent or grandparent. Some prophets may have these or other minor "warts and scars." Does it make any difference? We follow the prophets because they are the Lord's anointed and because God commands it. And there is no other alternative by which we can return to our Heavenly Father and enjoy all the blessings that are a part of his eternal kingdom. We should say, as did Peter when Jesus asked the Twelve if they too would desert him as nearly all others had, "Lord, to whom shall we go? Thou hast the words of eternal life." (John 6:68.) No matter how the sectarians interpret the Bible to make it say otherwise, it is a four-thousand-year-old testimony to the fact that the Church cannot exist and the work of God cannot go on without continuous revelation through living prophets.

To many nonmembers and, perhaps, to many members as well, it is too frightening to have another mortal tell us what God considers a sin. We don't want any one man telling us what we must do. Also, we don't want to be around another person who, if God so desires, has special powers to discern our thoughts and sins. But who else can we trust to have the keys of salvation? There are no others. Just as he gave the keys to Peter and the Apostles of old, the Savior has given our prophets those keys today. We certainly cannot trust anyone else. History and life around us are full of examples wherein mortals have led others astray into business failures, moral downfall, tragedy, and confusion. We cannot trust the well educated, nor the sophisticated, nor the controllers of our money, nor any other "greats" of any worldly pursuit.

We can trust only the Lord's chosen—chosen in the way that the scriptures prescribe. There are many self-appointed so-called prophets; but they always lead their followers into confusion, obscurity, and sin. They follow temporarily popular movements, or cling to the external trappings of some past movement instead of to the eternal truths. Only living prophets who are called by revelation, sustained by common consent, and otherwise approved by the Lord can guide us through the many trials and temptations that arise daily and yearly. They do not often follow popular trends; but they lead us carefully and safely through the process of perfecting the Saints, the work of the ministry, and the edifying of the body of Christ, the Church. (See Ephesians 4:11-16 and D&C 112.)

Those who are familiar with the scriptures, ancient and modern, and with history, secular and ecclesiastical, know that the prophets do not lead us into error. But even the wisest of men who have not received the gifts and callings of the prophetic office are rarely right about anything. Solon, a sage of high reputation in ancient times, said: "Like gaping fools we amuse ourselves with empty dreams. . . . Do not doubt it, insecurity follows all the works of men, and no one knows, when he begins an enterprise, how it will turn out. One man, trying his best to do the right thing, steps right into ruin and disaster, because he cannot see what is ahead: while another behaves like a rascal and not only escapes the penalty of his own folly but finds himself blessed with all kinds of success." (As quoted in Hugh Nibley, *The World and the Prophets*, Deseret Book Co., 1954.)

Another ancient philosopher said just about the same thing: "The hopes of men are often exalted in one moment only to be dashed down in the next, as they roll helplessly in a sea of false expectations and miscalculations. For no mortal man ever got an absolute guarantee from the gods that his affairs would turn out as he thinks they would. There is always some unknown quantity that vitiates any attempt to predict the future." (Nibley, *The World and the Prophets*.)

Several plays of the Greek author Euripides ended with the same declaration that seemed to sum up his cynical analysis of the unpredictable way of this mortal life. For example: "The gods take many forms. Indeed, they bring surprising things to pass. And that which we have confidently believed in goeth not unto fulfillment, while the gods manage to bring about the one thing that nobody expected. That's the way things are." (Nibley, *The World and the Prophets*.)

There is no guarantee of safety in this life through human plans. We are assured, however, that if we trust the prophets and follow them carefully, all things will work out in the end for our good. After the trials of this life are over, there is a reward for the faithful. And there are many good times in this life as well. In the not-so-good times, too, there is always the joy and contentment and peace of the obedient.

We can only trust a prophet of God to lead us through the great risks that threaten constantly. It is a great thing for the Church to announce that we are led by prophets as were the Saints of old. But our prophet is not obliged to prophesy of coming events. Nor is he obliged to answer questions to satisfy men's curiosity about this event or that dilemma. He speaks when the Spirit so moves him. He declares that which God reveals to him. He does not respond to public opinion, nor does he tend to do those things which would increase his or the Church's popularity.

We trust our living prophets, and we love them; but we do not worship either the living or the dead prophets. Once in an airplane I waxed eloquent to a fellow traveler over the accomplishments and greatness of the Prophet Joseph Smith. I recited his visions, revelations, translations from ancient records, organization of the Church, founding of cities, leading of multinational proselyting efforts, and so on. At one point my seat companion remarked, "I am very impressed with all you have told me about your prophet. Now I can see why you would erect such a great temple and tabernacle as a shrine over his grave."

I was startled by that comment and quickly explained, "Oh, no, he isn't buried under Temple Square. In fact, not many members of the Church even know where he is buried. I don't know myself."

My fellow traveler exclaimed, "You don't know where he's buried! But you worship him, don't you? Surely you have a great monument of some sort, a great temple, mausoleum, or cathedral, honoring him and containing his remains?"

I could see I had far oversold or distorted the honor we give our prophets. I said, "No, sir. You see, we love our prophets, and we obey them; but as each one dies, he is replaced by another so that we always have a living prophet.

"As a matter of fact, I do know where our second prophet, Brigham Young, is buried. His grave is in Salt Lake City in a small cemetery that was once a part of his estate. I have driven past his grave, but never have I gone into that little cemetery to pay homage to that great man. I have been to another cemetery not far from that one where several of our past prophets are laid to rest, but only as a member of the cortege on the occasion of their burial." After further discussion and emphasis I finally made my point.

We worship only God the Eternal Father. In a slightly different sense or degree we worship and honor each member of the Godhead; but we place the Father at the head, then his Only Begotten as his agent and our Redeemer. And in no way do we worship any prophet, whether ancient or modern. We do not pray to them or bestow a special sainthood on them. We do not believe they can intercede for us or that their good deeds contribute any merit from which we can borrow. We believe that all salvation and intercession reside in the person of Jesus. Only his atonement can satisfy justice. (See Acts 4:12; Mosiah 3:17; Helaman 5:9.)

We look back with respect on all the dead prophets and heed their teachings, especially any teachings or revelations which have become a part of our standard works. But it is the living prophet to whom we must look for guidance through the present events and circumstances of life.

Very few would argue against the idea that the friendship of God would be great capital. But many fail to see that we must be friends of the prophets to be friends of God. If you will read the Old Testament until you really begin to understand it, you will see that it is a several-thousand-year record of the fact that the "capital" (the spiritual reserve) of a people soon runs out when they reject and persecute the prophets. This turns out to be a fact literally as well as figuratively, temporally as well as spiritually. Those nations which persecuted and warred against Israel were brought down to poverty and obscurity one after another. And the Israelites themselves prospered in all ways when they carefully followed the prophets; but when they turned their backs on the prophets and utterly refused to repent, after a while God turned his back on them. Then they went down into a speedy captivity both temporally and spiritually.

The Lord has warned that rejection of the gospel and especially of the Book of Mormon will result in temporal and spiritual captivity and destruction for the great nation of the United States of America and all other peoples. (See 1 Nephi 14:6, 7; D&C 84:49-59, for example.) Poverty, slavery, and all their attendant horrors will overtake all those who trust in any "capital" other than that found in the friendship of Jesus and his friends. (See D&C 84:63-77; 98:1-3; 112:1-34.) If a man loves his friends, will he turn his back on them and support their enemies? Neither will God sustain the enemies of his friends. And we do not have to judge the worthiness of these friends of God, his anointed leaders on all levels. We can let God judge his friends. He will judge us by how we support his friends (whether or not they seem to deserve our support). We can trust him. This trust of him and his servants will store up eternal capital that will support us in the day of judgment.

Let me warn you that spiritual capital, like worldly capital, can be tainted through carelessness. As a banker, I learned that I must not be tainted by such things as bribes, bets, gifts, and favors. A banker who is effective cannot have a past that can be used against him. Even a bet on a horse race could come back to haunt a banker. It could be called *prima facie* evidence that he may be a "dipper"—one who "borrows" money that is not his own to cover unexpected gambling losses. To carry that over into the spiritual realm, let me ask a question: How appropriate would it be to have as General Authorities, stake presidents, and other leaders people who have been careless in their moral and business activities? True, we have repentance. Yes, I know about Alma the Younger. But it is a fact that such things have to be considered. And a spotless past *is* capital in a special sense. Again, I wish to add that the Lord and the Brethren are forgiving. Apply this principle to your future, not your past. Apply repentance to your past, but keep your future spotless. It is as important for a teacher of deacons to be spotless as it is for a General Authority to be spotless.

Fret not thyself because of evildoers, neither be thou envious against the workers of iniquity.

For they shall soon be cut down like the grass, and wither as the green herb.

Trust in the Lord, and do good; so shalt thou dwell in the land, and verily thou shalt be fed.

Delight thyself also in the Lord; and he shall give thee the desires of thine heart.

Commit thy way unto the Lord; trust also in him; and he shall bring it to pass.

And he shall bring forth thy righteousness as the light, and thy judgment as the noonday.

Rest in the Lord, and wait patiently for him; fret not thyself because of him who prospereth in his way, because of the man who bringeth wicked devices to pass.

Cease from anger, and forsake wrath: fret not thyself in any wise to do evil.

For evildoers shall be cut off: but those that wait upon the Lord, they shall inherit the earth.

For yet a little while, and the wicked shall not be: yea, thou shalt diligently consider his place, and it shall not be.

But the meek shall inherit the earth; and shall delight themselves in the abundance of peace. (Psalm 37:1-11.)

People often think thrift—accumulation of capital—is hard and is a deprivation. That is a shortsighted view of life. The self-control and effort are worth it. The saving time vastly improves the times that follow. So it is with spiritual capital: A lifetime of service and loyalty to God and his servants will result in an eternity of heavenly riches, a life with the Father in his kingdom forever, and all that goes with that.

CHAPTER SEVEN

Self-Control and Trustworthiness

Character, capacity, and spiritual capital depend primarily on the development of self-control. A person who is out of control cannot be trusted. Certainly the Lord will withhold trust from those who cannot control their thoughts, their language, and their behavior.

Toward the end of World War II, I entered the Navy's Flight Cadet Program. Flying Uncle Sam's airplanes was exciting and adventurous, but there were risks. Occasionally a cadet would make a mistake and "bend" an airplane. If he survived, he was required to write a report of the accident. In the report he usually admitted that he had forgotten something vital, such as to lower the landing gear, to add appropriate carburetor heat, to have sufficient reserve fuel, and so on.

One of my favorite true stories is about the cadet who did not want to admit that he had done anything wrong in spite of wiping out his own and three other aircraft. His accident report stated: "The *aircraft's* speed was too high on final approach. The *aircraft* hit the runway first with one wheel and then with the other.... It did a few kangaroos down the runway.... The *aircraft* swerved off the runway and across the grass.... It crossed the parallel taxiway... bounced across more grass.... The right wing hit a truck parked in the wrong place...and *then* I lost control and *we* cartwheeled into the three parked planes...." (Italics added.)

Obviously the aircraft was out of control from the beginning. The cadet must have had his head "down and locked," hiding inside the cockpit, while all sorts of things were going wrong. He had long since lost control of such essentials as airspeed, direction, and perception. He could have shut down the engine, used the brakes, or collapsed his own gear instead of running into things with the engine still pulling the aircraft along at fifteen hundred RPM. No one was in control at all.

In a similar attitude but with much more serious consequences, a young man came to see his priesthood leader and confessed a serious sin. But the young man thought that he should be allowed to continue as if nothing had happened because, he said, "It was an accident....I really didn't intend to do it."

Few active Church members really want to commit sins; but, at the same time, I don't think that very many, if any, of them sin accidentally.

In this case, when the leader probed deeper, he found that this young man's life was very much out of control. He was dating the same young lady much, much too often and was spending too many hours at a time with her too late at night, and they were going to the wrong places and doing the wrong things. They were "an accident waiting for a place to happen." Satan provided the place, and the "accident" happened. They were living too fast. They had lost control of their speed. They were going in the wrong direction. They were not doing the right things. They were not home at the hour their parents had asked them to be. They were not trusting in God and in his commandments to keep themselves pure. They were trusting in the "arm of flesh," which was sure to fail under the stress they were placing on it. They had begun to lose their virtue piecemeal. No one (except, perhaps, Satan) was in control at all. Yes, there was forgiveness to hope for; but the "accident" did damage that could be very difficult to repair. Even with all things eventually repaired (spiritually) through repentance and the Atonement, there is great risk in a situation like this that such things as character, self-confidence, and reputation may suffer damage throughout this lifetime.

Before any sin happens, the thoughts of the transgressor are out of control. "As [a man] thinketh in his heart, so is he" (Proverbs 23:7), or so he becomes. This is one reason why the Lord tells us that we are supposed to control our thoughts, and that if we don't control them, we will be judged and condemned, to a certain measure, by them as though we had committed the sin itself. Alma makes it very clear when he says:

"For our words will condemn us, yea, all our works will condemn us; we shall not be found spotless; and our thoughts will also condemn us; and in this awful state we shall not dare to look up to our God; and we would fain be glad if we could command the rocks and the mountains to fall upon us to hide us from his presence." (Alma 12:14.)

Can there be any doubt on the subject? In other words, we, ourselves, are responsible for the things we think. There are always those who want to pass this heavy burden on to someone or something else. But here it comes home to roost right where it has to be. We are the ones who must control what we think.

When we meditate a little on this subject, we come to realize why it is necessary for us to control our thoughts. Here is a little chain that is very revealing:

Thoughts become words.
Words become actions.
Actions become habits.
Habits become character.
Character becomes destiny!

King Benjamin had another way of saying almost the same thing. In his great sermon, he ends his declaration with this bit of philosophy:

And finally, I cannot tell you all the things whereby ye may commit sin; for there are divers ways and means, even so many that I cannot number them.

But this much I can tell you, that if ye do not watch yourselves, and *your thoughts,* and your words, and your deeds, and observe the commandments of God, and continue in the faith of what ye have heard concerning the coming of our Lord, even unto the end of your lives, *ye must perish.* (Mosiah 4:29-30. Italics added.)

Some people would argue with the idea that we are guilty just because we let our thoughts get out of control. They contend that the thoughts really are not a sin until the deed itself occurs. That is Satan's argument. But the Savior in the Sermon on the Mount points out that to look upon a person of the opposite sex with lust is to commit adultery in the heart. He is saying that the thought comes before the act. The body is but an instrument of the mind. The Savior, therefore, speaks of committing adultery in one's heart and implies that it is just about as bad as committing the act itself. For this reason he gave the higher law: that one should not even think immoral thoughts or imagine himself or herself in an immoral situation. He said, "Ye have heard that it was said by them of old time, Thou shalt not commit adultery: But I say unto you [and here he gives the higher law], That whosoever looketh on a woman to lust after her hath committed adultery with her already in his heart." (Matthew 5:27-28; see also 3 Nephi 12:27-29.) Today he may have said, "Whosoever looketh upon a person of the opposite sex to lust after them hath committed adultery with them already in his or her heart." This phrasing includes both men and women because it seems that in today's world there is just about as much sin initiated by women as there is by men.

Some psychologists even go so far as to say that nothing is an accident, that the thought comes before the action, whether good things or bad, whether intentionally or in error. They don't think a musician plays a wrong note without thinking he is going to first. They insist that even dropping a dish or tripping are caused by a subconscious thought that it might happen. So it does happen.

I don't think a bank robber would get very far with an argument that holding up the bank was an accident—that he just happened to be inside the bank with a gun, and he pointed it at the teller, and then he lost control and the words "*This is a stickup*" just kind of tumbled out without his really wanting them to. No one likes to get caught. All too commonly the defense is that "it was an accident." But in reality the thoughts were there; the established controls or restrictions were ignored or intentionally bypassed. Any sin takes thinking before it happens. The thinking can be guided by Satan, and it can be very subtle—pornographic advertising, immodest clothing, suggestive movies, immoral jokes, as well as the downright pornographic movies, magazines, novels, and so forth. Thus the thoughts get out of control long before the sin occurs.

We are the keepers of our minds. We can control our thoughts. Our minds are like computers: garbage in, garbage out. If we let impure things into our minds, then impure things in the form of words or actions will surely come out. We will be judged for letting garbage in instead of beautiful, uplifting, inspiring thoughts that edify our minds. When the memory banks of our minds are perfectly recalled at that great and final day of judgment, many of us are going to be much embarrassed by the images that appear on the screens of our minds. (See 2 Nephi 9:14.) We will want to hide when we see the garbage that is there. If we have not repented and partaken of the Atonement, every dirty joke enjoyed, every nasty thing, every pornographic magazine, picture, movie, novel—every dark and ugly thing that we would want to hide will be restored to our complete awareness, to our shame and disgrace. We probably thought that they were all behind us. But that day will cause us to cringe unless we truly have cleaned up our acts and our minds while in our mortal probation. That means that we have repented and asked for forgiveness; that we have put clean and uplifting and spiritual and cultural things into our minds; that we have sought good things from the best books; that we have anxiously tried to improve our minds and the quality of our thoughts; that we have sought beauty and culture and inspiring gospel ideals; that we have tried to fill our minds with thoughts of the Savior and the kind of thoughts he would like us to have. If our repentance is genuine, our minds will be purified and we will see fear depart. Jesus is the sole judge. (See 2 Nephi 9:41.) And he knows all our thoughts and the intents of our hearts. Wouldn't it be better to have beautiful jewels of thought for him to see, rather than the garbage some show him?

Parents should be anxiously providing the motivation and the opportunity for elevating and cultural reading or entertainment. Although the Church helps, it is the responsibility of the parents to set the patterns and habits of reading, movie going, and TV watching of their children. But as children reach the age of accountability, nothing can remove their individual responsibility for what goes into and what comes out of their minds. This is another reason why the scriptures advise us to read "out of the best books." (D&C 88:118.)

Elder Boyd K. Packer has told us that we can control our thoughts by putting spiritual thoughts in place of the gray or dirty-black thoughts that might come into our minds. He helps us remember that the light will replace the dark. If we substitute a scripture or our favorite spiritual hymn that we have memorized, the imps on the display screen of our minds will slink away. Of course, it takes self-mastery; but that is exactly what life is all about. We must control our actions and our thoughts. That is central to the test of this life. In nearly every conference address, President David O. McKay urged self-control not only as a means of realizing our goals in life, but also as the main purpose of mortal life itself.

Our characters will be judged more by what we say about others than by what others say about us. We must control our tongues. Our use of words, our vocabulary, our control of our phrases, largely serve as a basis by which others come to know us and to measure our value and our character. Again, Alma says it very clearly: "Our words will condemn us." (Alma 12:14.) James also powerfully accuses those who cannot keep their tongues in control:

> If any man among you seem to be religious, and bridleth not his tongue, but deceiveth his own heart, this man's religion is vain. (James 1:26.)

> For in many things we offend all. If any man offend not in word, the same is a perfect man, and able also to bridle the whole body.

> Behold, we put bits in the horses' mouths, that they may obey us; and we turn about their whole body.

> Behold also the ships, which though they be so great, and are driven of fierce winds, yet are they turned about with a very small helm, withersoever the governor listeth.

> Even so the tongue is a little member, and boasteth great things. Behold, how great a matter a little fire kindleth!

> And the tongue is a fire, a world of iniquity: so is the tongue among our members, that it defileth the whole body, and setteth on fire the course of nature; and it is set on fire of hell.

> For every kind of beasts, and of birds, and of serpents, and of things in the sea, is tamed, and hath been tamed of mankind:

> But the tongue can no man tame; it is an unruly evil, full of deadly poison.

> Therewith bless we God, even the Father; and therewith curse we men, which are made after the similitude of God.

> Out of the same mouth proceedeth blessing and cursing. My brethren, these things ought not so to be.

> Doth a fountain send forth at the same place sweet water and bitter?

> Can the fig tree, my brethren, bear olive berries? either a vine, figs? so can no fountain both yield salt water and fresh.

> Who is a wise man and endued with knowledge among you? let him shew out of a good conversation his works with meekness of wisdom. (James 3:2-13.)

> But the wisdom that is from above is first pure, then peaceable, gentle, and easy to be intreated, full of mercy and good fruits, without partiality, and without hypocrisy. (James 3:17.)

One of the attributes of the great Church leaders I have known is that, even though they are uniformly men of strong willpower and strong opinions, they speak no ill of anyone. If they cannot say something good about a person, they don't say anything at all. In their positions they come to know the weaknesses and sins of many people, and they would have a lot of gossip or "juicy" information to pass on. They honor their sacred trust, however, and speak only the best about everyone. It is also true, however, that there are occasions on which they rise to righteous indignation for just causes or against sin and error per se. Some leaders are terribly eloquent when preaching against sin and Satan. But all the leaders I know fear ever doing or saying anything that would diminish the reputation of any person, good or bad. Their love for the sinner and their abhorrence of sin is the clue.

Rumor and gossip do terrible damage to innocent people. Many who pass on unfavorable information are on ego trips. Because of a poor or twisted self-image, they just can't resist letting someone else know that they know—that they are "in the know," that they are privy to something secret that only "important" people know. Somewhere they have picked up the erroneous idea that talking negatively about someone else—passing on something startling or shocking—will enhance their own image in the eyes of the hearer. Such is not the case, yet the trend continues on. Only the spirit of the gospel can reverse this trend, and even then progress usually comes slowly. Gossip is a disease of young and old alike, both male and female. Words, like feathers in the wind, cannot easily be picked up after having been released. The damage is done too quickly. The place of control is inside our own minds. If we don't have the thoughts of gossip, we won't have the words. If, due to our position, we know of something negative, we must learn to control both mind and tongue so that nothing slips out. In either case, it still is a matter of control—self-control. That is still the test.

Profanity is also a matter of tongue control, but it is different from gossip. Profanity is a matter of habit and of lack of adequate vocabulary to express frustration, emotion, passion, and so on. Ultimately, the strong feelings need to be controlled.

If one works in an environment where nearly everyone uses gross swear words, it takes more self-control to avoid adopting the same words and phrases than if one works in a cultured and refined environment. The problem can arise from within the home too.

Children tend to use words they hear their parents use. They also pick up the worst words from other children on the playground. If the parents place enough emphasis on clean, good words, the children will learn what is appropriate and what is not appropriate. But the main emphasis of parents should be not just to cover up naughty words at home but to help their children eliminate such words from their vocabularies.

I spent a few years in the navy, where I was subjected to the most foul language. Yet these expressions never became part of the vocabulary of some of us because we never allowed the thoughts and words to become a part of us. It requires a conscious effort to keep them out, and also an equally conscious effort to have proper substitute phrases ready. Part of the problem is simply maturity. Most of us grew up wanting to impress the bigger guys. As soon as we noticed that the "big guys" used some dirty language, we thought we could show how big we were by using the same words. Some grew up to the point at which they realized that the "biggest guys" did not necessarily use bad language. Some clean-speaking heroes also came into our lives. But some just never did grow up, and they are still trying to impress someone with how "big" they are by showing, in fact, how small their vocabularies are.

I was not attracted to vulgar language because of the following experience: My father died when I was about six. He has remained a hero to me through all the years of my life. Everyone always spoke highly of him. I was proud to be his son. Inevitably the day came, when I was about eleven or twelve years old, that I wanted to impress the older boys with my use of some raw, ugly words. I thought about them and rolled them around on my tongue to get used to them. If my mother had heard me use them, it would have meant a heavy dose of pepper, to be sure.

I waited for an opportune moment when no adults were around. A bunch of the guys were sitting on the running boards of two cars side by side and talking. The right moment occurred and I made my cheap little statement with the dirty words designed to impress the most jaded of them. At that very moment one of the men of the little town walked by. Because of the way the cars were parked, I had not seen him approach. He went on by as though he had heard nothing. I sure hoped he hadn't. A few moments later he came back on the other side of the cars, and this time he called to me. "Hi, Bobby, can I see you for a moment about something for your uncle?"

Relieved that there was no embarrassing scolding, I followed him away from the group and out of hearing distance. Then he looked me in the eye and said, "I heard that, Bobby. Your father wouldn't have liked to hear that from you." Then he left. It cut me to the quick. No chastisement could have inflicted more pain. He was very wise in that he had not tried to "cut me down" in the sight of those I was trying vainly to impress. I might have rebelled at that. Instead, he hit me right where I was the most vulnerable. And to this day I shrink and cringe at the thought of that moment or any other moment in which I might use words which would adversely affect the trust of my father, my mother, the prophet, or anyone else—especially my Savior.

There are many ways to be vulgar and profane; and there are words and phrases in which the name of the Lord is taken in vain. One little community I know of found nothing wrong with using two common four-letter words. But they were horrified at the people in the next little town down the road where they did use, with some frequency, the name of deity but would never lower themselves to use the two common words heard in the first town. Each looked with equal condemnation upon the other. Both were wrong. Neither can be excused. It was all an unnecessary habit. But I mention it since, in matters of profanity and in the use of the name of the Lord in vain, many people frown upon the words of others but never notice their own sins. Their own lack of vocabulary has caused little bad habits to form, and they don't even notice that they profane or swear. Clean it up. Ask others for help.

Each of a pair of friends, teenage young men, asked the other to help in wiping out the habit. When a bad word was noticed, the friend could slug the offender on the shoulder muscle as hard as he could. It was a manly kind of game and it worked. A few bruises and each had cleaned up his mouth.

President Spencer W. Kimball, a saintly prophet and manly man, was being wheeled into the operating room by a young orderly. The young man unfortunately smashed his finger between the metal bed frame and the metal door frame. It hurt and it bled. The young man let out a popular oath in which he took the name of the Savior in vain. The prophet, somewhat sleepy from the sedatives already administered to him in anticipation of the operation, opened his eyes with difficulty, looked at the young man, and said, "Oh, please don't say that. He is my best friend!" The chastened orderly, rebuked in love, apologized and ceased. Do we have enough love of the Savior that we

could do what the prophet did? Would we defend the sacred name of
the Savior from misuse? Would we do it with quiet love?

Just like an airplane, the emotion called anger can get out of
control. For our own good and the good of those about us, we need to
learn to control this emotion or passion. Some throw a tantrum,
others just rant and rave, while some seem to seethe inside. It is true
that control is naturally easier for some than others; but whatever the
price, anger is one thing that just has to be controlled if we are going
to seek the celestial kingdom. The Savior again gave the higher law by
which we are to be guided. It, along with other higher laws he gave at
the same time, is in the Sermon on the Mount. As the author of the
law of Moses, as Jehovah of the Old Testament (before he was born of
Mary), it was the Savior who engraved the Ten Commandments on
the tablets of stone. Therefore, the Savior, as the agent of the Father,
had the authority to give a higher interpretation of the Ten Commandments. He told the multitude, as recorded in 3 Nephi:

> Ye have heard that it hath been said by them of old time, and it is also
> written before you, that thou shalt not kill, and whosoever shall kill shall
> be in danger of the judgment of God;
> But I say unto you, that whosoever is angry with his brother shall be
> in danger of his judgment. And whosoever shall say to his brother, Raca,
> shall be in danger of the council; and whosoever shall say, Thou fool,
> shall be in danger of hell fire. (3 Nephi 12:21-22; see also Matthew
> 5:21-22.)

A lot of people make the mistake of saying that the law of Moses
was a harder law than the gospel. The law of Moses was sterner with
reference to the practice of punishments and the daily control of lives.
But the gospel is a more difficult law to fully live up to, as the above
passage shows. Jesus does not just ask his disciples to refrain from
murder, he also asks them to refrain from anger and from using angry
and derisive epithets. This requires control. Note that the 3 Nephi
sermon carries some important differences as compared with the
Matthew version. Some scribe perhaps inserted the words *without
cause* in the Matthew version. Everyone would like that, for everyone
thinks he has cause for anger. Even the child beater thinks he has
cause. The abuser of animals thinks there was just cause for pain he
inflicted in his anger. Such activities—striking children, spouses, and
animals in anger—perhaps are why the Book of Mormon carries the
different words. There must be no question that God does not

countenance an unbridled temper. Just as lust is the father of adultery, anger begets murder. So lust and anger must be expunged from our systems before they grow up to be the full-blown sins. It is another matter to "reprove sharply [intelligently] when moved upon by the Holy Ghost." (D&C 121:43.) Uncontrolled anger is a human emotion, not a divine one.

If we expect to associate with God, angels, prophets, and peaceful people in a celestial atmosphere, we will want to be people who are not given to loud outbursts of wrath. While on earth we will learn to control thoughts, words, and actions; and we will learn to conduct ourselves in a manner that would be appropriate in such sacred company. We will make our homes and our offices that way now. And we can. Now is the time and place to adopt the spirit of those great hymns "School Thy Feelings, O My Brother" and "Let Us Oft Speak Kind Words to Each Other."

Strong emotions, such as being angry and feeling offended, are a poison to the spirit. A person who suffers from attacks of these emotions will quickly lose the Spirit. They just do not go together. Satan uses these emotions to destroy us and to do his work. It is usually noted that a person who harbors a grudge against another for offenses (real or imagined), or one who feels offended, or one who is angry at another, stops coming to church. Such people do not seem to enjoy spiritual things. The negative emotion consumes their spiritual desires. The spirit of vengeance and punishment and retribution takes over in their hearts and minds, and they lose the Spirit of the Lord. In fact, this is why we must never give up attending sacrament meetings: going there induces us to forgive, because we cannot go on partaking of the sacrament in hate.

These negative feelings are a poison. We should react to them as we would to the bite of a poisonous snake. If a rattlesnake slinks along the ground and bites my foot and then flees, what should I do? Should I pick up a stick and then look for the snake to punish it, or should I get the poison out of me as fast as possible? Surely, I should get the poison out quickly! Just so with being angry and feeling offended. I should get the poison out immediately. Never should I think of punishing the offender. That will do no good. I am more in danger than the offender.

This concept is somewhat foreign to the thinking of most angry or offended people. They usually want to attack and punish the offenders. I remember a story about a man who came charging into a Church leader's office, red in the face, neck veins bulging, and demanding, "You've got to call so-and-so to a Church court. You've got to excommunicate him. You must punish him!"

The leader already knew something of the problem between the two men, so he answered, "You sound like he has offended you rather seriously."

"He sure has," was the immediate reply.

The leader then offered, "Brother, let me read a scripture to you."

The offended brother rejected the idea, saying, "Read it to him, read it to him!"

The leader tried to get through to him, saying, "Well, you ought to hear it first." He started to read Doctrine and Covenants, section 64, verse 9: " 'Ye ought to forgive one another; for he that forgiveth not his brother his trespasses standeth condemned before the Lord.' "

Here the offended brother interrupted, saying loudly, "Read that to him. Read that part about being condemned before the Lord. I like that."

"No, no, you don't understand," said the Church leader. "This is for you. It says, 'He that forgiveth not his brother... standeth condemned before the Lord; for there remaineth in him the greater sin.' "

In other words, the one who feels offended and does not forgive the other has lost the power of the Atonement until he forgives. His past sins have come back on him, and he still carries their guilt—the greater sin. He easily could be worse off than the offender, who may have meant no offense in the first place. Few who feel wronged can understand this; but it is very clear. He who has the strong negative emotion of feeling offended, of feeling wronged, of feeling anger, has the poison. The one guilty of the offense may have his own sin to account for, but the one feeling offended has to get rid of the poison quickly—without waiting to punish the offender—before it kills his spirit. One can get the poison out by forgiving, forgetting, over-looking, making excuses for the other person, understanding human frailties and idiosyncrasies, not worrying about petty accuracies, realizing that the other person probably made an error, and so forth. "Also take no heed unto all words that are spoken; lest thou hear thy servant curse thee: For oftentimes also thine own heart knoweth that thou thyself likewise hast cursed others." (Ecclesiastes 7:21-22.)

To say, "I forgive, but I won't forget," does not get the poison out and does not do any good. The old grudge and the miserable misunderstanding between neighbors or between relatives and in-laws or between brothers and sisters in the Church are terribly sad for all concerned. Again, the solution is for the offended one to forgive and forget. It is the only way the Lord will be lenient on him for his offenses. As we judge others, so we will be judged. The more forgiving we are, the more forgiving the Lord will be with us.

Most offenses are imagined anyway. People may occasionally say unkind things that hurt, but even then it usually was not intentional but just thoughtless. One philosopher said, "To be insulted over something the other person did not intend as an insult is foolish. To be insulted over something the other person did intend to be an insult is doubly foolish because the other person has the greater sin until you get into the act, being offended or insulted, and take upon yourself the still greater sin of not forgiving."

In a South American branch a girl was doing her best to play the little foot-pump organ. It was an old instrument, and she was struggling. Then her mother heard another sister make the disparaging remark, "That organist isn't worth much." The mother felt offended and took her daughter by the hand, and they left without saying a word to anyone. After a week had passed without anyone seeing the mother or her daughter in church, the branch president called at the home to see if there was any sickness. The mother, still tearful over the incident, declared to him that she would never return while that other sister was still there. The branch president visited the second sister, who denied ever having said anything derogatory. The branch president then had the job of getting the two ladies together, which he finally accomplished with great difficulty.

The mother told again how her daughter had been insulted and how, after all, the young girl was doing the best she could.

The other sister suddenly put her hands to her face in anguish as she remembered the situation. "Oh!" she exclaimed. "Oh, no! You mean you think you heard me say that the organist, your daughter, wasn't worth much?"

"That is exactly what you said," retorted the mother.

"What a terrible mistake!" the lady replied. "What I really said was, 'The *organ* isn't worth much.' It is old, and we need a new one. I am very, very sorry you misheard or misinterpreted me, but I would never say one word against your lovely daughter and her playing ability."

Witnesses were found who could verify the conversation and things were resolved. But how often are innocent people offended by innocent remarks, and then they never get together to straighten matters out? What a tragedy! If the offended one doesn't come forward, the offender may never know what the other person thinks he heard. There are many variations on this subject. The only reasonable solution is for an offended person to forgive and forget—to get the poison out, to control his emotions, for his own good and everyone else's.

This chapter has been a rather detailed recitation of the day-by-day hard little things that we must do to pass the highest test of this life: the celestial test, you might say. In reciting them, I do not mean to discourage anyone. As is everyone else, I am grateful for the Atonement. I am grateful for the promise in Mosiah 26:30: "Yea, and as often as my people repent will I forgive them their trespasses against me." Without that hope in Christ, we all would be lost. But the other side of the coin is that our efforts must be sincere. Some may have further to go, but their faces must be pointed in the right direction. That is a basic part of repentance. It is a turning around of one's life, an acceptance of Jesus as our Redeemer and our only hope of salvation, and then a constant putting of one foot in front of another until we have plodded right into the kingdom, the everlasting one.

We may wish for heroics that can, in one big jump, take us all the way into heaven. But it is a step-by-step thing, a constant learning of details. Let me fall back on my flying experience for an illustration.

I have been flying many kinds of aircraft for the last thirty years, both in the United States and in Latin America. Once when I had returned to the States after an absence of some years, a very dear friend offered me the use of his new twin-engine Cessna. It just happened to be one of my favorite airplanes. It not only had the special, powerful engines with turbo superchargers which could take it up to very high altitudes, but it also had all the radios, all the electronic navigational aids, the transponder, the distance-measuring equipment, full instruments for all-weather flight, oxygen, and so forth—just like a commercial airliner. I couldn't think of a more enjoyable plane to fly; but with so much equipment, such a very expensive, sophisticated bird, I reluctantly passed up the chance to fly it, saying, "Someday we'll go to Mexico together."

A few months passed, and every time I saw my friend he offered his plane again; but I never felt I should accept, even though the offer was very sincere. Then one day my friend brought a set of keys and a pilot's manual to my office as evidence that he really would be pleased if I would use his beautiful aircraft at some time. The keys in my hand generated an overwhelming desire to go down to Mexico to a favorite spot. Unfortunately, my friend couldn't go the days I had free, but he assured me that I should go alone. We discussed my qualifications of being covered under his insurance policy; and it turned out that I needed a check ride with a qualified inspector, as it had been some time since I had flown that particular type of plane.

The arrangements were made, and I met the inspector at the side of the airplane at the appointed hour with my licenses issued in the United States, Argentina, Paraguay, and Ecuador, and with log books showing flights in Cessna 310s across jungles, mountains, deserts, and international boundaries. He smiled calmly but seemed unimpressed and said, "I've heard about you, and I have no doubt about how much flying you have done, but I have to assume that those flights were when *nothing* went wrong. Now let's fire up this bird and see how well you fly it when *everything* goes wrong!" For the next hour he made everything go wrong that conceivably could go wrong! He simulated every emergency he could think of. He turned things off that should have been on. He turned things on that should have been off. He tried to create disorientation or panic. He really wanted to know how well I could fly when everything did go wrong! In the end he climbed out, signed my log book, and announced, "You're okay, I'd let my wife and kids fly with you." I took that as a great compliment. I had passed a test.

I tell you this story as an illustration. This life is a sort of check ride. I hope that when I meet the Lord he will reassure me that I did all right even when everything went wrong here on earth. And I hope you are performing that way while everything is going wrong in your life. And to return to the metaphor that launched this book, that of the banker, if you are living the little day-by-day unglamorous things—the things that wives and mothers do, the things that faithful fathers and responsive children do—you are putting money in the bank and extending your credit line. You are building *trust*.

CHAPTER EIGHT

The Rewards of Trust in God

Paul said that "faith is the substance of things hoped for, the evidence of things not seen." (Hebrews 11:1.) If this is true—and of course it is—then it follows that faith is a measure of trust in God. Out trust and faith can be measured by how long we are willing to wait for the rewards of trust. They also can be measured by how great a test we can survive. Let me illustrate with an example of each of these two measures of faith and trust.

The first story incorporates the principle of tithing. Stories about this concept most frequently tell of obviously miraculous demonstrations of short-term financial improvement that compensate for the tithing paid (the convert gets a promotion at work when he begins paying tithing, the payer receives a payment of a debt he had long since written off) or of a dramatic rise in economic circumstances. Such blessings certainly qualify under the well-known promise in Malachi 3:10. But what of the tithe payer whose means never rise above the modest level but who feels himself nevertheless to be richly blessed? After all, the Lord can bless in many ways.

This story is about such a situation. It begins in the first few years of this century. Ann, aged about twenty-two, and her widowed mother were living alone in a small rented house in southern England. The two women and Ann's fiancé had joined the Church a year or two previously; but in those days the teaching of investigators was not what it is now, and in any case tithing was not emphasized in the way it quite properly is today. These women were aware of the principle, but nothing more. They lived in very poor circumstances anyway, having to rely on the inadequate income Ann earned from working hard and for long hours at a factory, and from the two women taking in washing (which of course was done by hand in those days). They "knew" there was no money for tithing.

One evening a woman came to see them who had lived in the branch earlier, immigrated to Utah, and was now returning on a visit. As they talked of the Church and what it meant to them, the subject of tithing came up, and the woman bore her testimony of the principle. It sounded wonderful. But how could they pay one-tenth of their small and uncertain income? "We couldn't afford to pay tithing," Ann and her mother told the woman.

The visitor reacted excitedly. "Don't tell me you can't afford to pay tithing," she said, her voice rising as she struck her fist on the table. "You can't afford *not* to pay tithing. Trust the Lord's promise, and you'll never regret it."

The challenge was clear, and the two women rose to it. They set aside as the tithing bank a can which had a lid, and they placed the meager tenth in it whenever they received any money. There was no sudden rise in living standards, certainly no dramatic increase in income. But over the weeks and months they began to see that the Lord's mathematics were operating to somehow make the nine-tenths go as far as the ten-tenths had previously.

When Ann and Bert married, and throughout their lives, the practice continued. Times were still hard at first, and the couple was supporting the widowed mother, but things slowly began to improve. Soon the family moved from their poor neighborhood to a slightly better house—still rented, of course. They would never be really prosperous, never even save any money, but the couple raised three children, paid their bills, and served in the kingdom.

Successive moves brought them finally to Utah in their sixties. When they died, they left no material property—they never owned a home. But they felt themselves richly blessed and always bore strong testimony to the principle of tithing and of trusting the Lord's promises. Their three children, now grandparents, are active in the Church, have always been firmly committed tithe payers, and have taught their children the same principle.

This simple but somehow profound story has undoubtedly been

repeated thousands of times all over the Church and all over the world. It seems to me that such people have been blessed in wonderful, long-term ways as they have put their trust in the Lord's promises.

Of course, we must pay tithing freely. It must not be begrudged, or paid in the spirit of testing God. We must remember that the Lord and his kingdom on earth do not need funding as much as the members need the blessings. He could reveal the location of the veins of gold, the deposits of emeralds, the fields of diamonds, and the location of the oil-bearing structures, indicating exactly where to drill. But such is not the way of the Lord. His divine decree is that *we* are to be blessed, not the Church. (Without us, there is no Church.) And the way we individually are blessed is by living the commandments.

Many faithful tithe payers will testify of their blessings in obeying this particular commandment. When we really trust the Lord by tithing promptly and exactly, by tithing off the top when the salary is received or the profit has been realized, the blessings usually come just as promptly. If, on the other hand, we wait until the end of the pay period to see if we have enough left over (not really trusting the Lord), we seldom, if ever, have anything left over. Satan and circumstances see to that.

The setting for my second illustration of trust and faith—the one that involves magnitude of trust—is the Mormon colonies in Mexico during the time that Pancho Villa was plundering and murdering his way through that part of Mexico and even across the border in the United States. To appreciate the scope of this trial of trust, bear in mind that the colonies were a logical target for Villa on which to vent his hate for Americanos and in which to replenish his ever-scant rations. Also, bear in mind that flight and self-defense are powerful human urges.

Pancho Villa was a leader of a Mexican political party. There was a civil war between his party and other parties. The United States gave a military advantage to one of the groups against which Pancho Villa was fighting. The United States allowed the other army to come into the States and move around behind Pancho Villa's army, where they did serious damage to Villa's forces. This apparent help by the United States caused Villa to retaliate against the closest Yankees he could find. He attacked cities across the border and killed some Americans. He then returned back into Mexico, still furious and determined to kill all gringos he could find. In his path was the large Mormon colony, all gringos to the general, and his intent was to wipe them out too.

At this point I would like to continue the story by quoting from the diary of W. Ernest Young:

> Villa spent about two days at the Coralitos Ranch, and while there he executed a few Mexicans just because they were employees of an American company. I knew some of them, the Pavela brothers, two fine-looking men. Including the American miners at Santa Isabel and Minaca, and the several ranchers on his way to Columbus, and the twenty-four in Columbus, some forty Americans had been killed.
>
> At Washington, President Woodrow Wilson was busy negotiating with the Mexican government to find a way to punish Villa. They finally reviewed history of a deal that was carried out to punish the Apache Indians when Geronimo committed depredation on both sides of the international border back in the 1880s. This deal permitted either government the right to cross the border when in hot pursuit of the Indians. It was then that General John J. Pershing was appointed to enter into Mexico with a punitive expedition of some 15,000 soldiers. He was restricted in not being able to use any railway nor occupy any towns.
>
> The Presidency of the Church in Salt Lake City had communicated with Phillip H. Hurst in El Paso regarding the dangers of our people, especially those in Dublan, and we had been notified of the attack at Columbus. President Anthony W. Ivins, knowing the territory and having traveled many times over the roads, knew what might happen when Villa's army had already murdered helpless ranchers.
>
> The Mexican government was committed to aid in this business of capturing Villa, but the soldiers from Chihuahua were slow in taking part, and secretly it looked as if no real effort was put forth to accomplish real help, which thus gave Villa time to escape into the fastness of the mountains. Villa was also helped by the local people who would not divulge information regarding his whereabouts. . . .
>
> With little or no communication, we were left very much to our own judgment as to what course to pursue. President Joseph C. Bentley was at Colonia Juarez sixteen miles away. If any definite instructions were given regarding what should be done, Bishop Anson B. Call did not report any, and then, who could know what Villa's plans might be? It was a very serious matter, and we were in great fear. Bishop Call met most of the men in Dublan in the street in the center of town near the stores. His counselors, Nephi Thayne and I, stood near him. Two opinions were voiced, to make an exodus to the mountains or to go to the small garrison at Nuevo Casas Grandes for protection. Bishop Call as our leader had the right for inspiration, and he finally told us to go to our homes, turn out all lights, and retire with a trusting faith that the Lord would answer our prayers.

Villa and his army must have left the Coralitos ranch near midnight. They arrived at the north end of Dublan about 3:00 A.M. and stopped. Villa remarked that Carranza must have sent more soldiers to defend the place. His subalterns said they saw no reason for this. Villa persisted and swore that the place was occupied by a force of men and that there were lights, etc. This is what the two local Mexicans I knew testified that they heard Villa say at this time, but they themselves did not see an army nor any such military activity. Both Maximiano Rubio and Roberto Salgado were capable men, and their testimony is trustworthy. Several of our own men heard them testify to this effect. I knew these two men of Colonia Juarez, as did Alma Walser [the father of sister Helen Walser Wells, wife of the author] and Joseph F. Moffett, who heard their testimony. It has been stated that a prairie fire might have reflected lights on the windows of the houses to cause such a condition, but in March the land is very barren and any brushfires would have been too far away for this.

Many prayers were invoked by people far and near, and President Anthony W. Ivins was fasting and praying at the Salt Lake Temple at this time. Bible history gives testimony of divine intervention, and Villa at this time was diverted in his course when he ordered his men to turn left and beat a new road over the prairie and travel on to Chocolate Pass some fifteen miles to the southeast. No doubt, Villa's soldiers would like to have continued their pillage and murderous acts. On March 22, Bishop Anson B. Call presided at a Thanksgiving assembly in Dublan to render thanks to the Almighty for his divine intervention. (Copyright 1973, Walter Ernest Young. Used with permission.)

Now that this is all history, it is easy to see that a miracle occurred. But try to imagine yourself there that night in the streets of Dublan. Would you have followed the counsel of that bishop? He hesitated a long time and then calmly said, "I am going home to pray. Then my family and I will turn out the lamp and go to bed." There were some protests. Some wanted to flee and others wanted to take a military stand, as they were tired of being pushed around by the North Americans and now the Mexicans. But one calm soul stood up and announced to everyone, "I am going to follow the example of the bishop. I am going home to hold family prayer and then we will turn out the lamp and go to bed." One by one the others present decided that the best thing to do was follow the bishop. It was a great trial; but their trust was rewarded.

Some dramatic examples of the rewards of trust surface continually in the mission field. We send many thousands of missionaries out annually—enough to have over thirty thousand in the field constantly. Only a church that can ask for everything could do this.

Only a people motivated by pure love and prompted by the Spirit would make this sacrifice constantly and with hardly a single murmur of complaint. Only such a people as ours would "go where you want me to go" as the hymn says. ("It May Not Be on a Mountain Height," *Hymns* no. 75.) All the words of that song are an inspiration to the Saints and are worthy of repeated study. Mind you, we don't say, "Johnny, where would you like to go on your mission, and how long would you like to stay?" We say, "Johnny, your mission call is to South Africa for a year and a half," for example. Or he is called to Hong Kong or Denver—maybe even Salt Lake City. And he has little or no say in the matters of where or how long. Sometimes the call seems illogical. But time almost invariably verifies the inspiration behind it, as the following stories illustrate.

Two missionaries were impressed to stop at a certain house and ring the door bell. Normally when a person responded, they would give a "door approach." This time, however, when a lady opened the door, they stood silent, unable to say a word. Without speaking, she looked at one and then the other and back again. Then she said, "Yes, you are the ones. I've been waiting for you—please come in." Inside, she explained, "I saw your faces in a dream eighteen years ago. I've never forgotten. Over the years others in white shirts have passed by my door, but I was waiting for you. You are the ones with a message for me. What am I to do?" She was baptized in a few weeks.

When one of these missionaries next saw his mission president he asked, "Why did you send me to such and such a city?"

The mission president said, "I don't really know. That is just what the Spirit seemed to indicate."

Then the missionary asked, "And why did you assign me to work with Elder Smith?"

Again, the mission president indicated that he had no particular reason except that it seemed to be the right transfer to make.

The missionary then told the above story and added, "President, do you realize that I was only two when she saw me as I now appear? Do you realize that, if you had assigned any other elders to that area, she wouldn't have been baptized, because she was waiting just for us? President, what if my girl friend had been successful in getting us married. Or what if the coach had been successful in getting me to accept the scholarship to play ball this year? I wouldn't have been here, and she wouldn't have joined the Church."

Of course, he is not entirely right in implying that the Lord relies on chance. In his infinite foreknowledge, he knew what would happen and prepared for it without interference with free agency. (See Alma 13:3-7.) But the missionary's comments illustrate the desirability of trusting in the Lord.

As a missionary, part of trusting the Lord is believing that there is a very special work to do wherever the mission president assigns us. The same trust is exercised in acceptance of the call. Every missionary has a date with destiny in the mission to which he or she is called.

A European missionary expected to be called to serve in a European mission. He spoke several Scandinavian tongues and a little English. Others from his country had been called to serve in their home country or neighboring countries. But, to his great surprise, when he opened the envelope from the prophet with the Salt Lake City postmark, he found that he was going to a South American country. He trusted in the Lord that there was a special reason for him to be the first from his country to go so far and to have to learn an entirely new language. He went to the Provo language training center and then off to South America. After a few months with a North American companion, the mission president assigned him to work with a local Latin companion. Part of the idea was to help the European missionary learn Spanish better.

The first week together a strange thing happened. They went to send their mail at the post office, and the European companion noticed that the Latin companion was requesting stamps to send his letter to his parents in Europe. Not only that, he saw that the address was to the same city where his own parents lived. What a coincidence! On further inquiry, he found that the South American missionary's parents had been exiled for political reasons and had moved to Europe. They were nonmembers. The European companion's parents were members of the Church, and they lived only a short distance from the South American companion's parents. Arrangements were quickly made for the member parents to visit the nonmember parents and invite them to their home, to church, and so on. In a short time the good news came back from Europe that the South American's parents were joining the Church. What inspiration! The prophet did not know why he was calling a Swede to serve in Chile. The mission president did not know the Chilean missionary's parents were in Sweden. Only the Lord could have put it all together.

A lovely young lady had suffered a sad accident in her youth. Although she was very beautiful, part of her face was paralyzed. Her friends and family hardly noticed her handicap; but it made her feel insecure and created an inferiority complex. Because of her misfortune, she feared that she would never find a husband. The time came when she was old enough to be allowed to go on a mission. She felt that there was some way for her to help others in the service of the Lord. There was no indication in her missionary application form that she had this facial paralysis, since it did not affect her ability to serve in any way; and the picture of her face in repose reflected the very pretty girl she is to all.

The prophet assigned her to serve in one of the almost two hundred missions there are in the world—a South American mission. When she arrived at her mission headquarters, she found that the mission president's wife had suffered from exactly the same kind of malady from her youth. She learned that this mission mother had overcome the feelings of inferiority, the lack of self-confidence, and whatever other complexes she had built up in her youth, and had made a beautiful life for herself. And, obviously, she had found a good man for a husband, had raised a lovely family, and now together each was serving a second mission. Her mission mother was happy and self-confident. This helped the lady missionary gain self-confidence and hope and faith in the future. She also knew that her assignment to that particular mission was not just a coincidence.

There is an LDS businessman who travels occasionally by plane. His personal missionary technique is to sit down next to his seat companion and say, "Hello. Do you know who I am?"

The stranger usually says, "No, who are you?"

The member then states, "I am probably the only man you know who can tell you how to avoid divorce when you or your wife die!" That is startling enough to lead to a good conversation that will last quite a while—usually to the destination and sometimes until baptism.

That story, in a rather dramatic way, calls attention to this businessman's correct perspective of things and his trust in the Lord. He knows that Joseph Smith told the truth. This leads him to the conclusion that all the keys, powers, dominions, thrones and glories are a logical result of acceptance of the restored gospel. He trusts God to sustain all the eternal things. All earthly trials and hardships as well as all earthly blessings are transient experiences, a part of the joys and sorrows that make up mortality; though of course their effects can be lasting. Missionaries who persevere in trusting the Lord, gradually come to realize the tangible, sometimes dramatic rewards of their labors. This businessman-missionary has a correct perspective on the world because of his trust in the Lord. He partakes of the spirit of Doctrine and Covenants, section 128:

> Now, what do we hear in the gospel which we have received? A voice of gladness! A voice of mercy from heaven; and a voice of truth out of the earth; glad tidings for the dead; a voice of gladness for the living and the dead; glad tidings of great joy. How beautiful upon the mountains are the feet of those that bring glad tidings of good things, and that say unto Zion: Behold, thy God reigneth! As the dews of Carmel, so shall the knowledge of God descend upon them!
>
> And again, what do we hear? Glad tidings from Cumorah! Moroni, an angel from heaven, declaring the fulfilment of the prophets—the book to be revealed. A voice of the Lord in the wilderness of Fayette, Seneca county, declaring the three witnesses to bear record of the book! The voice of Michael on the banks of the Susquehanna, detecting the devil when he appeared as an angel of light! The voice of Peter, James, and John in the wilderness between Harmony, Susquehanna county, and Colesville, Broome county, on the Susquehanna river, declaring themselves as possessing the keys of the kingdom, and of the dispensation of the fulness of times!
>
> And again, the voice of God in the chamber of old Father Whitmer, in Fayette, Seneca county, and at sundry times, and in divers places through all the travels and tribulations of this Church of Jesus Christ of Latter-day Saints! And the voice of Michael, the archangel; the voice of Gabriel, and of Raphael, and of divers angels, from Michael or Adam down to the present time, all declaring their dispensation, their rights, their keys, their honors, their majesty and glory, and the power of their priesthood; giving line upon line, precept upon precept; here a little, and there a little; giving us consolation by holding forth that which is to come, confirming our hope!
>
> Brethren, shall we not go on in so great a cause? Go forward and not backward. Courage, brethren; and on, on to the victory! Let your hearts rejoice, and be exceedingly glad. Let the earth break forth into singing. Let the dead speak forth anthems of eternal praise to the King Immanuel, who hath ordained, before the world was, that which would enable us to redeem them out of their prison; for the prisoners shall go free.
>
> Let the mountains shout for joy, and all ye valleys cry aloud; and all ye seas and dry lands tell the wonders of your Eternal King! And ye rivers and brooks, and rills, flow down with gladness. Let the woods and all the trees of the field praise the Lord; and ye solid rocks weep for joy! And let

the sun, moon, and the morning stars sing together, and let all the sons of God shout for joy! And let the eternal creations declare his name forever and ever! And again I say, how glorious is the voice we hear from heaven, proclaiming in our ears, glory, and salvation, and honor, and immortality, and eternal life; kingdoms, principalities, and powers! (Verses 19-23.)

The above glorious message from section 128 should galvanize every trusting Latter-day Saint into action. Whoever would collect the rewards of trust in the Lord must first learn to trust. I believe most people would do better than they do if they just knew how. Perhaps we need to nag people less and try harder to tell them *how* to improve. That is what I have been trying to do in this book. I have tried to explain how trust works between a banker and a borrower, for instance. I think that analogy can be helpful to everyone if they realize that temporal things, seen in a true light, are also spiritual things. The same actions, beliefs, and attitudes that will make you a better risk to a banker will make you a more trustworthy disciple of Jesus. If you increase your day-by-day working character, capacity, capital, and control, you will also increase these qualities in all spiritual realms and operations. I merely suggest that you keep this analogy in mind and try to apply it so that you may live safer and *trust* more wholeheartedly.